BURIED IN HAMF

Each in his narrow cell for ever laid,
The rude forefathers of the hamlet sleep.
(Gray's *Elegy in a Country Churchyard*)

When properly conducted, genealogical investigation teaches much about the vicissitudes of life; the vast extent of human oddness.
(Anthony Powell, *Infants of the Spring*, 1976)

View from Hampstead Parish Churchyard, looking towards St John's Wood, by T.M. Baynes, 1822.

BURIED IN HAMPSTEAD

A Survey of Monuments at
Saint – John – at – Hampstead

by

Camden History Society

reported by
Christopher Wade
and photographed by
Terence Nunn

Camden History Society
1986

SOME RELEVANT DATES

986	King Ethelred's Charter, giving Hamstede to the Abbot of Westminster
1312	First evidence of a chapel on site of present church
1551	Hampstead manor passed into lay hands
1560	Church's burial registers begun
1745–7	Old church, dedicated to the Blessed Mary, pulled down. Present church built and named St John-at-Hampstead.
1796	Lysons surveyed Hampstead's monuments
1812	Additional Burial Ground
1814	Park's *Topography and Natural History of Hampstead* included some grave inscriptions
1830s	Many cemeteries opened (1839 Highgate)
1843–4	Church enlarged with transepts and westward extension
1852	Burial Act (London) closed Metropolitan graveyards
1854	Order in Council ended most burials under church and closed old churchyard
1855	Burial Act instructed Burial Boards to maintain closed churchyards 'in decent order'
1876	Hampstead Cemetery opened
1878	Church enlarged and re-orientated, accommodation for 1,444 people
1878	Further Order in Council again prohibited burials under church and in old churchyard
1881	Millward recorded monumental inscriptions
1884	Cremation legalised, after interval of 1,100 years
1912	Building of Choir Vestry caused some tombs to be moved (architect, Temple Moore)
1959	Footstones (and all except headstones) abolished
1961	Hampstead Borough Council assumed responsibility for maintaining churchyard
1964–5	Building of Crypt Room displaced more monuments

BURIED IN HAMPSTEAD

© 1986 Camden History Society

ISBN 0 904491 22 6

Printed by Printpoint Ltd., London
Typeset by Phoenix Photosetting, Chatham

CONTENTS

INTRODUCTION

Hardly had we begun our survey in Hampstead Parish Churchyard that summer afternoon in 1976, when a smartly uniformed schoolgirl paused on her return home and asked us what we thought we were doing. Delighted to explain, our reply was full of new-born enthusiasm about the recording of inscriptions, but it was cut short by the girl's very superior interjection: 'Isn't that really rather a *silly* thing to do?' As we gasped, she pointed to the tombstones and added: 'After all, they won't go away!'

How we would love to meet again our teenage critic and show her that even during the eight years of our survey some of the inscriptions have, in fact, gone away. Pollution, vandalism, rain, ivy, old age, have all taken their toll – a sad fact which was the main reason for our survey in the first place. Most London graveyards have been closed to new burials for many years and, where their tombstones have not been broken up for crazy paving, or ranged like dominoes round the walls, they have suffered a rapid decline. The need to record Hampstead Parish Churchyard was becoming more and more urgent.

Another reason for our survey was that our Society had recently completed and published its researches into *The Streets of Hampstead*, which had naturally unearthed a large number of noteworthy residents, and we were keen to follow them up after they had gone to ground in 'God's Acre'. We could see why Family History Societies consider churchyards as 'yards of history'.

Tombstones are particularly helpful and usually reliable about dates of birth and death, and about family relationships: some inscriptions cover three or four generations of a family, and some graves grouped together reflect the consanguinity of their inhabitants. Furthermore, many people who chose to be buried in Hampstead must have been either long in residence or much in love with the place, and that added to our interest in them. The long residents included a few famous names and also more importantly, many old Hampstead families, and all the unsung butchers and bakers and staymakers (and other past professions) who had serviced Hampstead over the years. Among those who came and saw and succumbed to its charms was none less than John Constable, who exclaimed about Hampstead: 'Here let me take my everlasting rest.'

We soon realised that there was much more to be learned than local history and biography. Here was social history – attitudes to life and death and the hereafter, in varying styles of poetry and prose; art history, ranging from Georgian symbolism, through Victorian sentimentality, to twentieth-century reticence; some basic geology, distinguishing between limestone, marble, slate, granite, sandstone, Cragleith, and other curious stones; and incidentally some natural history, surrounded as we often were by flowers and trees and cats and the best of British birds. We could tell those of our friends, who looked on graveyards as deadly dull, that we were working in a sculpture park, set in a nature reserve, recording white plaques, which were much more informative than blue plaques, and which included Constable, du Maurier, Gaitskell and other household names. They suddenly became more interested.

It would not have taken us eight years to complete our work if the problem of Burgh House had not blown up in 1978. This meant that the editorial staff of the graveyard survey had to divert their energies to help to save one of Hampstead's finest Queen Anne houses for community use, and to launch the Hampstead Museum there. We had

The tomb of John Constable and family.

originally hoped to publish our results by 1981, as that was exactly a century after the inscriptions had nearly all been recorded by a Mr Millward. His transcripts, pencilled into exercise books, which were invaluable in our operation, had miraculously been preserved, and can be seen in Camden's Local History Library: they are reported in more detail elsewhere in this book.

Our main Graveyard Group consisted of Vivien Binn, who also typed the 88-page index of Millward's work; Dr Barbara Ely, Geoffrey Harris, Shirley Harris, Deirdre Le Faye, who also devised the large-scale maps; Alison and Terry Nunn, who also photographed many of the graves; and Christopher and Diana Wade, who together edited the entire survey. Further recording was done by Catherine Browne, Nora Franglen, Jane Hammond, Eileen MacDonald, Beryl Moss, Susan New and Jane Speake.

Our grateful acknowledgments of help begin with Camden's Local History Librarian, Malcolm Holmes, and his staff, who gave us material and moral support throughout. Documentary assistance and background information at the church came from Wilfred Hill, John Brandon Jones, Dionys Moore, Ted Nugee, Maggie Willmer and Inigo Woolf. Martyn Pedley of the North London Polytechnic gave us geological advice about tombstones, and Cyril Corden, the funeral furnisher, helped us with monumental masonry. We had further assistance from Doreen Crooks, Christina Hinkley, Cherry Lavell, Jim Pike, Peyton Skipwith, Julia Smith, Mary Speers and Sir William Wade. The Vicar, the Reverend Graham Dowell, gave us his blessing.

Christopher Wade
Hampstead
January 1986

View of the Old Church at Hampsted.

'View of the old church at Hampstead'. This engraving shows the mediaeval building, which was replaced in 1745–7 by the present church.

I. CHURCH AND CHURCHYARD

In 1986, as this book goes to press, St John-at-Hampstead is celebrating one thousand years of worship in Hampstead. There is no mention of a church in the Charter of 986, wherein King Ethelred the Unready gave the manor of Hampstead to the monks at Westminster, but the community was there, and it is presumed that the monks would have provided it with a place of worship.

Hampstead's mediaeval church, dedicated to the Blessed Mary, is shown in an old engraving (page ◀) to be a picturesquely irregular structure of assorted styles, with high-pitched roofs. The style of the east window suggests a date of about 1220–40, and there is documentary evidence to show that a chapel existed here by 1312. In the early eighteenth century, when Hampstead became a fashionable spa, this building soon became too small for the local congregation. As a petition to Parliament in 1710–11 put it: 'Hampstead being a place of great resort, especially in summertime, the said church, were it in a reparable condition, would not be sufficient to accommodate one half of the parishioners', noting further that the church was in such a dangerous condition that 'the inhabitants could not attend Divine worship without apparent hazard to their lives'.

After several dangerous decades, the old building was torn down in 1745 and the present church erected, dedicated to St John; but as nobody is sure which John, patronal days are celebrated for the Evangelist *and* the Baptist, and both saints appear in the west windows. The later history of the building is described in the church guide and other publications, and need not be repeated here, except to note the enlargement of 1878, which entailed the complete re-orientation of the church. The chancel and altar are now at the west end of the building which, apart from St Peter's in Rome, is very rare indeed.

The crypt beneath the chancel contains a number of tombstones displaced from other subterranean vaults. The custom of allowing the richer members of the congregation to be buried under the church was discontinued in the mid-nineteenth century, when their malodorous presence began to offend the rest of the congregation. An Order in Council of 1854 prohibited such burials, but four vaults with later dates can still be seen in the crypt (not open to the public).

The present graveyard round the church is on a mediaeval site and is the oldest surviving unspoiled churchyard in the centre of Greater London. Most others have been cleared or tidied into parks or playgrounds. Hampstead remains romantically unstructured, attractively sloped and well wooded. This unfortunately makes problems for graveyard recorders and for the churchyard maintainers who, with the financial aid of Camden Council, have to prune, mow and generally try to keep the whole 'in decent order'; this was the phrase used by the 1855 Burial Act about the maintenance of closed churchyards.

The old graveyard was officially closed by another Order in Council in 1878, two years after Hampstead Cemetery was opened at Fortune Green, but there have been a few later burials in plots and vaults already purchased. Several tombstones on the south-west side of the church were re-sited in 1912, when the choir vestry was built, and more were moved in 1965, when the Crypt Room was constructed.

The south east corner of the 1812 extension with the graves of (L-R) the Llewelyn Davies family, Anton Walbrook, the du Maurier family and Hugh Gaitskell.

Across Church Row, an extension was opened in 1812, and laid out in a convenient grid pattern. The rows are lettered A–Q from west to east, and numbered 1–110 south to north. The numbers are cut into the stone on the western wall. The area between No. 1 and the southern wall is officially called the Bay, thus the du Maurier grave is numbered I Bay, and Hugh Gaitskell is I 1. For the extension (but not for the older yard) fairly accurate records have been kept of who is buried where. The north-east corner (Rows L–Q) was used only from the 1930s and includes the so-called Columbarium or cloister, with its wall bearing commemorative plaques, and a small memorial garden. These features were prompted by the increasing demand for post-cremation memorials. The extension has some fine old trees and, in the north-west corner, some flowering shrubs and other garden delights contributed by a nearby resident.

Lamenting the general apathy towards the maintenance of monuments, Frederick Burgess in his splendid *English Churchyard Memorials* (1963) comments: 'These stones are indeed vulnerable, subject to the quixotic changes of English weather, to air pollution . . . and to man's charity, as fickle as a vane!' With Hampstead churchyard officially closed, and ever fewer graves tended by relations, the church has a major problem in repairing the many damaged tombs. Few families have provided funds for this purpose, and many have left the district. The Gardnor tomb (XB 011) near the main gates has now happily been restored in memory of a local parishioner, but many others need urgent attention if this part of Hampstead's heritage is not to crumble away.

Caroline White in her *Sweet Hampstead* (1901) said of the old graveyard of a hundred years ago:

> The flowery garden-graves, the close-mown turf, the shrubs and bowering trees and the varied, often elegant tombs amongst them, give Hampstead churchyard an air of beautiful repose and quiet.

Many of these pleasures have fortunately survived, but much is now in danger.

II SYSTEMS AND SOURCES

On a good day, recording a graveyard can be rewarding detective work in beautiful, flower-filled surroundings, under the shade of the old yew trees. On a bad day, the stones prove indecipherable, the brambles scratch and scar, and the yew trees drop their berries, ruin your clothes and wreck your notes and drawings.

We started with a good day, choosing to begin in the churchyard extension, where the graves are easier to identify and the inscriptions easier to read. Our initial equipment was a clipboard and a supply of recording forms, which we had specially devised for the occasion. We had studied forms published by archaeological and genealogical organisations (see Bibliography) and pitched ours somewhere between the two.

Our main interest was in the local history we could extract from the inscriptions and how it related to the other local surveys we had undertaken. We wanted to learn more about the people who played an important part in the life of the town. This would include parsons and publicans, schoolmasters and vestrymen, rich men in their mansions and tradesmen at their gates. Half of the front of our form was reserved for inscriptions, and all of the back for biographical notes. At the same time we had to describe the tombstones, in order to guide enquirers, both present and future, to the source of our information.

The form asked for the material and condition of the stone, and for a rough identikit sketch (with height) of the grave for easy recognition. We also photographed all of the near 2,500 graves, which had something of interest to show. As it was, the photographer often found it difficult to catch a stone in the right light to make the inscription legible.

Finally, the form had a section for notes on random interests, such as calligraphy, names of masons and artists, cross references to other family burials, footstones and directions (which side of a stone was inscribed).

Each grave was given a reference number, as shown on the map in this book. In the new graveyard, we used the official grid numbers, A 1–110 etc. (see description in Section I), and gave V numbers to some isolated vaults near the gate to the Parochial School. Where a memorial was missing, but the inscription had survived from an earlier recording, the nearest grave numbers were shown e.g. E 3–4. In the old churchyard, patches divided by paths were labelled XA, XB etc. Monuments in the church were numbered, clockwise, starting at the back of the nave, with the prefix CH, while CR meant crypt. Plaques in the Columbarium were on north or east panels and referred to as Col. N, or Col. E (thus Col. E 3 indicated the 3rd panel on the east side).

Our recorders' graveside kit rapidly grew from the clipboard stage to include secateurs and trowel for uncovering graves, scrubbing brush and cloth for cleaning stones, and mirror and torch for reading faded inscriptions. A side light, from either sun or torch and angled by a mirror, would often bring out the eroded letters.

Millward

We had other sources of help for the older stones, notably Millward. In 1881, Robert Hovenden, FSA, an antiquarian living in Croydon, commissioned Mr Millward (we think his Christian name was James) to record all the Hampstead inscriptions: he supplied him with twenty-one ruled exercise books and paid him a penny a tomb. Millward lived with his son, Richard, who was headmaster of the Hampstead Parochial School and therefore

Symbolic skulls seen in the old graveyard on the Hart/Carey tomb of 1717 (left) and the headstone of Zechariah Bleake, who lost two wives in the 1720s.

occupied the school house, right next to the graveyard extension. Fortunately, the twenty-one books of inscriptions have survived in a bound book, which is now at the Local History Library in Swiss Cottage. This volume bears the bookplate of Thomas Barratt, author of *The Annals of Hampstead*, but was presented to the library by Kenneth Brown in 1934. Included in the book is Millward's final account for all the tombstones he read and his quantities can be usefully compared with those in our survey, which were almost exactly double:

	Numbers of stones	
	1881	**1984**
Old ground	743	825
New ground	442	1554
Church	46	96
Crypt	16	23
Totals	1247	2498
at 1^d per stone = £5.3.11		
small brush	4	
pencils	6	
Total	£5.4.9	

Millward's survey included many tombstones which have now disappeared through decay, damage or overburying, also many inscriptions which are now largely illegible. From his notes, however, we could identify a much eroded stone and, from his sequence of recording, we could fairly assume where a certain grave had been. We have logged all these inscriptions in our survey, although now there is often nothing to see on the grave but grass. Sometimes there is a new monument, showing that the plot has been re-used. A blank grave could also mean that the owner could not afford a memorial.

Snell and Lysons

A few years after Millward (no date is given), a Mr L.B. Snell recorded some (or all?) of the graveyard and sorted the inscriptions into alphabetical order. Only four volumes, covering the letters A, B and P, have survived at Swiss Cottage Library, which is especially tantalising, as some of his transcripts seem more careful and convincing than Millward's.

First in the field of our graveyard recorders, however, was the Rev. Daniel Lysons, whose survey of *The Environs of London* appeared in 1796. This included a not very reliable list of tombs in the churchyard, giving names, rank and dates, and sometimes a little biographical detail. He noted only one monument in the church, that of Anthony Askew, which he said was at the west end: it is now at the east end (CH 1). Lysons also said that the communion table was then at the *west* end, whereas the church guide suggests it was at the east end until 1878. John Rixton's tombstone in the north aisle was also mentioned: being dated 1658, this was and is the oldest surviving inscription.

Sundry Sources

Two local historians who included some helpful graveyard jottings in their publications were John James Park (1814), and Thomas J. Barratt (1912), but each was limited in scope by an elitist name-dropping tendency.

Two Manorial Surveys of the eighteenth-century shed some welcome biographical light on darkest Hampstead: we found many of our names in the Particular of 1703/4 and the Field Book of 1762 (both in Swiss Cottage Library). The latter survey gave details of the properties occupied, all shown on the manor map.

In the graveyard extension, we were able to give names to grassy patches by consulting the Sexton's List, which has entries for most graves on a row-by-row basis. In the old churchyard, we were helped by a manuscript map of some of the graves (undated but about 1860), which was found in the church archives. We consulted the Burial Registers in order to check some names and dates, and we noted all the addresses form 1940 onwards, where Street Directories could no longer assist us. But we had to restrain ourselves from transcribing all the registers (they go back four centuries and have now been microfilmed), which is another operation. We asked for information in the Parish Magazine, especially about design and biography, and had at least two replies.

Puzzles and Blunders

When all our sources had been exhausted, and even Millward had written 'illegible' about a stone, we spent much time trying to coax some information from the faded inscriptions. Most old stones began with 'Here lieth the body of . . .' or 'Sacred to the memory of . . .', which gave us an idea of the style and quality of the lettering. Names could be solved like crossword puzzles. If you could read a few letters like -A-T-- -RE-N, you might guess it was MARTIN GREEN and then confirm it by identifying the missing letters. The same system revealed some interesting professions, though ME-------- ENG-----ER was guessed as MECHANICAL ENGINEER and turned out (from literary sources) to be MEZZOTINT ENGRAVER.

Dates and ages were highly confusable. The figures 1 and 4 could look alike, as could 3 and 5, 6 and 8, and so on. Some of Millward's dates had to be checked and revised, for instance, where he gave a succession of family burials which suggested that a lady's children were born several years after her death. In another case, the dates of birth and death were 130 years apart. Other problems in eighteenth-century stones were old spelling, e.g. 'Here lyes ye body of . . .', the use of the long *s*, which looks like an *f*, and masons' abbreviations, where January became Jany, dangerously similar to June.

For many months we believed all the facts we found on tombstones, until we gradually realised that stonemasons could make monumental blunders. In the case of the Rev. James Castleden (XI 009), a local Baptist minister, who died in 1854, aged 76, it may not have been the mason's fault, but the stone asserts that he died in 1855 aged 72. It was certainly a masonic error to spell Jane Austen's relations (XB 211) 'Austin' (but this has been corrected) and to worry us all over TIRAMIET.

One of the finest decorated tombs (XE 061) in the whole churchyard is that of Mr William Hart, 'late Citizen and Salter of London', who was buried in 1717, and was joined in 1751 by Robert Carey Esq, 'Tiramiet Merchant'. The fact that Carey was spelt with an E, whereas his widow, here called a relict, and daughter were spelt Cary, did not disturb us. We found many such variations on the older tombstones, together with a vagueness in later years about hyphenated surnames. But where or what was Tiramiet? We explored world gazeteers (with special reference to Tirana in Albania) and encyclopedias (was it a sort of sugar or spice?) and drew blank. We checked and rechecked the inscription, which was just legible in a good light, and pored over our recorder's stone-rubbing of the word. Her researches in the Guildhall archives had shown that Car(e)y traded with Virginia, so was it perhaps a sort of tobacco? Then she saw the answer. By putting the two words above each other, as written in the cursive lettering of the time:

T I R A M I E T

V I R G I N I A

she showed how the mason's brief, or the slip of his chisel, had caused the confusion. Robert Car(e)y Esq was a Virginia Merchant. (Unless, that is, some reader knows all about the Tiramiet trade?)

Footstones, which were officially abolished in 1959, could be helpful with names and dates. They usually gave the deceased's initials and year of death and, where a headstone had eroded entirely, this could identify a grave. In one case (XD 206), Millward gave the name on a very worn headstone as Mary Eastwood, but the footstone clearly said M A 1789, and the name had to be Astwood. Unfortunately, many footstones had lost their heads; being small and mobile, they could easily become displaced and often got dug into the wrong grave. By checking initials and dates, we could sometimes return these wandering stones to their home ground.

However worn inscriptions were, or initially baffling to read (we had several in Latin, French and Russian), we would pay them several visits and look at them from different angles. Some were clearer in low sunlight, others in shade, some with dirt on them and others with moss, which helpfully grew in the lettering; some had to wait until winter, when the grass and foliage died down. In many cases, we realised that if we did not read them now, they would be gone for ever.

William Hart and Robert Carey

End Products

When all the two-and-a-half thousand or so forms had been typed, they converged on the editors, who spent the best part of a year checking, re-typing, re-drawing and generally homogenising the information.

A further editorial concern was biographical research. Few personal details were included in inscriptions (any such details were underlined in red on the form), and one of the main interests of the survey was to find out more about the people buried here, especially those with local connections. Some of the results of our combings through *Who Was Who* and other biographical dictionaries, together with local histories, street directories, local press (especially obituaries), specialised libraries (e.g. Victoria and Albert), and our Local History Library, can be seen in a later section.

There is much more biographical material in the complete set of the final version of our forms, which has now been deposited with the Local History Library at Swiss Cottage. These forms, some of which are accompanied by photographs of the tombstones, can be consulted there on application to the library staff. With the forms is an index of the seven thousand or so names which appear in the inscriptions. These include the names of many relations, who are not buried in Hampstead. Copies of this index have also been deposited at the Parish Church and made available to the Society of Genealogists.

15

Our other end products are the six maps, which show the location of every grave or monument mentioned on the forms: the same reference numbers are used. In the new graveyard, the names are shown in a simple grid pattern. In the old yard, the different types of grave are shown by symbols for headstone, chest tomb, ledger, etc. Major trees and bushes are indicated, as these are aids to location. A number of missing graves are shown (with names in circles), near to where they were last seen. One set of maps has been given to the Local History Library, another to the Parish Church.

Finally, for those in a hurry, we have prepared three Tomb Trails to act as a short guide to the more memorable monuments. We hope that all our efforts to demonstrate the delights, interests and curiosities of the churchyard will encourage the local community to think deeply about its conservation.

The chest tombs of John Harrison (front) and Stephen Guyon (rear).

A corner of the old graveyard near the south door of the church, 1937. The artist, Randolph Schwabe, who has signed his drawing on John Harrison's tomb (see page 16), is buried in the churchyard extension. (Reproduced by kind permission of Alice, Lady Barnes, and the Fine Art Society).

Family Crests

Atkinson	XE 040
Bleamire	CH 20
Burn	XB 158
Cartwright	CH 80
Churchey	XE 086
Collings	CH 67
Dalgardno	XE 112
Davidson	XB 202
Douglas	XD 162
du Maurier	I Bay
Duncan	CH 13
Errington	CH 75
Erskine	CH 5
Fincham	XB 107
Fitzgibbon	XB 069
Gardnor	XB 011
Haldimand	CH 59
Hanson	XD 141
Holford	CH 62
Hood	XB 003
Houlditch	XG 028
Johnstone	XE 139
Lambe	A 6
Levett	CH 95
Macirone	D Bay 3
Merry	XD 009
Rixton	CH 52
Shaw	XB 128
Taverner	N 60
Thompson	I 91
Thomson	XD 081
Warren	XB 024
Wentworth	M 104
Woodd	XD 200
Woods	CH 56

Notable Names

Among the curious names found in inscriptions and listed below can be seen the strong influence of the biblical and Puritan tradition. Other reasons seem to be family names, place names, literary leanings and Nelson's victories.

Several inscriptions included nicknames, such as Bobo, Nibs and Tinker – and an unsolved curiosity attached to a married couple, 'Buckling and Skung', (M 106, George and Dorothy Carney)

This list is in order of birth: where the sex is not clear M or F appears in brackets

1658	Onyxia Swinburn, XE 123
1693	Bloomer Ireland (M), XE 135
1731	Philadelphia Hancock, XB 211
Early 18c.	Temperance Thornton (F), XB 034
	Blanchard Coward (M), XH 007
	Armine Snoxell (M), XG 028
1750	Zachariah Foxall Darby, XC 003
1753	Rejoyce Foot (F), XB 087
1760	Zephyrette Hyndman, XE 029A
1780s	Fountain Elwin (M), XE 015
1796	Albinia Skerrett, XB 141
c. 1800	Nehemiah Southwell Price, E 48
1801	Henry Paramour Ashenden, D 37
1804	Senthill Lindsay (M), D 3
1806	Horatio Nelson Abraham, A 50
1815	Horatio Beaumont Binns, XD 146
1835	Idonea Purton, XC 007
1850	Rymer Oyston Watson (M), D 97
1856	Stroud Lincoln Cocks (M), H 55
1875	Hephzibah Harriet Flux, L 107
19 c.	Hercules Robinson, E 23

Professions from other parishes found in inscriptions of 1770+

Upholder in St Paul's Churchyard[9]	1770
Cutler of Castle St, Leicester Fields[10]	1773
Soapmaker of St Giles[11]	1776
Builder of Leather Lane[12]	1778
Bookbinder of St Martin-in-the-Fields[13]	1778
Distiller of St Andrew's Holborn[14]	1778
Itinerant Linen Draper[15]	1780
Surgeon of Bolton St, Piccadilly[16]	1780
Tea Dealer of St Andrew's, Holborn[17]	1782
Tallow Chandler of Leather Lane[18]	1784
Wax Chandler of Old Bond Street[19]	1789
Builder of Snow Hill[20]	1792
Coach Maker of Long Acre[21]	1796
Lorimer (harness-maker) of King's Mews[22]	1801
Gunmaker to His Majesty[23]	1801

III RESULTS AND REWARDS

Raised Numbers relate to the list of graves at the end of the chapter, which gives relevant names and reference numbers

1. The People

'The churchyard is as beautiful and secluded as it is ancient', wrote Edward Koch in an SPCK guide to Hampstead Parish Church in 1928. 'The number of famous dead who rest in it is exceeded by none in the country.' The Reverend Koch's slight exaggerations can be explained by the fact that he was at one time the church's Assistant Curate.

The attractions, however, of being buried in these delightful surroundings, and of rubbing skeletal shoulders with so many great and glorious personages had long been well known. The main evidence of this was the number of people choosing to be buried here who, as far as we can tell, had nothing to do with Hampstead at all. An additional consideration from the eighteenth century onwards was that the City's graveyards were becoming overcrowded and insalubrious, and many people preferred the picturesque rurality of outlying villages, such as Hampstead. Though marriage in a church was always restricted to those of established local residence, no such rule evidently applied to burials, and the fees involved were doubtless welcomed by the vicar and the sexton. Metropolitan graveyards were finally closed by the Burials Act of 1852, which had been prompted by the grisly revelations of a Drury Lane surgeon.

Among the earliest surviving inscriptions from our churchyard (the stone has disappeared) is one of 1706, recorded in 1814 by J.J. Park, for Edward Jones, Printer in the Savoy (XL 021). Other early eighteenth century burials from the City area – mostly with surviving stones – include a 'currier (leather dresser) and citizen of London', who died in 1719[1]; a 'citizen upholder (upholsterer) of St Mary le Strand', 1727[2]; a distiller of St Bride's, 1729[3]; a pavior of St Martin-in-the-Fields, 1739[4]; and a woollen draper of St Dunstan-in-the-West, 1743[5]. Nearly illegible is the stone of Charles Smyth of Smyrna, Constantinople Merchant, who died in 1755 (XB 100).

Non-Hampstead

The main influx of burials from central London, however, began in the 1770s – a laceman of Long Acre[6], an apothecary of St George's[7], a hosier and hatter of St Andrew's, Holborn-above-Bars[8], and so on. A list is appended of other professions and locations that have appeared on our tombstones, apart from those included in our biographical section.

The most distinguished non-Hampstead person to be buried here in the 1770s was **John Harrison**, inventor of the marine chronometer, and popularly known as 'the Man who discovered Longitude' (see biography section). Harrison, who died in 1776, lived long in Red Lion Square, but no adjacent churchyard was evidently available to accommodate him. Extended researches in 1976, at the time of his bicentenary celebrations, revealed nothing to connect him with Hampstead, so he or his family must have chosen his final resting place (XE 007) at random, though obviously affected by the charm of this particular churchyard.

John Hall, mercer of New Bond Street, who lost wife and baby in 1777.

The wife of John Williamson, hosier and hatter of Holborn, 1776.

A view up the old graveyard with the vast Lewer family vault in the foreground.

In his *Annals of Hampstead*, Thomas Barratt tells the tale of a wealthy City merchant, **Henry Lewer** of Pimlico, who wanted a country walk one summer's day around 1800, and finished up in Hampstead. 'Arrived there, he sat down to rest on a tombstone in the Churchyard and, as he surveyed the scene, was so much struck with its beauty and the extent of the view that he resolved that "if he could not become a resident of Hampstead in his lifetime he would make it his last resting place when dead".' He instructed his solicitor accordingly, and his vast family tomb in the south-east corner of the old churchyard records in letters of stone (now badly flaking) that 'the whole is endowed and provided for in trust in the 3 per cent reduced annuities, 1817'. A further sum was set aside to pay for the funeral feast of each member of the family. In the grave (XB 190) are Lewer and his wife, six sons and their wives and children, a grandson or two, and some housekeepers. None of them had any living link with Hampstead.

Given the large number of interlopers, proven and non-proven, in our graveyard, it is clearly difficult to draw any major conclusions from our survey about Hampstead's past population. While much churchyard recording aims at revealing social trends and demographic patterns for a community, our findings do not lend themselves to statistical analysis or deep sociological evaluation. This is, perhaps, a mercy, as the attractions of numerical results are often outweighed by the dangers of generalisation. (We have seen a suburban graveyard survey report, based on 62 graves, declaring that 76% of the male population was called William.)

We have, however, learned more about old Hampstead families, including those who have left their names on local streets and property – Benham's Place, Burgh House,

Carlile Estate, Fenton House, Gardnor House, Guyon House, Holford Road, Monro House, Moreland Hall, Pilgrims Lane, Platts Lane and Willoughby Road. Also here are Kippin the sweep, whose cart has been preserved at Burgh House; Bert and Becky, our late Pearly King and Queen; the widow of Admiral Barton, who was thought to have lived at Admiral's House (but never did); and Stamp, the chemist, whose shop name has survived, unlike the legion of Crockers and Potters, who have all disappeared in the changing world of Hampstead.

The results of our survey may not shed a blinding new light on Hampstead's history, but they illuminate and illustrate many lesser-known corners of the community, and produce some notable nuggets of social history.

Dying young

The death of an infant is often the first inscription on our eighteenth and nineteenth century tombstones. The family then bought a plot, and gradually filled up the grave. There are many stones recording two or three children dying young, and a few with even greater bereavement.

In the mid-eighteenth century six of the Bettger children (XD 031) died under six years of age, and the Depost family (XE 058A) lost six under seven. Four of Sarah Hart's children (XD 120) died in infancy, her husband died aged 30: she lived to 81. Within ten years (1861–71), the Walters family (XB 019) lost Frank, aged 1, Edith, 6 months, and twins Ella and Beatrice, aged 1 month. 'Gladys and Lilian, twin daughters of F. and A. Escott, died 1918, aged 22 years' (I 26). Somehow the losses seem sadder when the children are named. Some parents used the name of a dead child for another child – the name was usually the father's or mother's – only to suffer another death. Eliza Payne (XB 031) lost two daughters successively named after her, one aged 3 and the other 7. Some stones give no details of young children's deaths, merely adding to the parental inscriptions, 'also 5 children of the above' (XB 156), or 'likewise 8 children in their infancy' (XD 146).

There is no evidence of multiple deaths from epidemics. It is known that Hampstead was spared from London's cholera outbreaks in 1832–3 and 1849, after which the New End Dispensary was built in gratitude. No cholera victims were found in the graveyard, although Barratt claims that an old lady from St Giles died from this disease in 1847, mainly because she took against the pure Hampstead water and had jars of St Giles water brought to her daily from the polluted church pump.

Living long

As a counterweight to records of infant mortality, note was taken of those who survived to a ripe old age. Spinsters were splendidly successful. In the mid-eighteenth century, the three Lister sisters (XB 040), each called Mrs, not Miss, died aged 72, 75 and 89 respectively. They were beaten by four Dove sisters (XB 093), who lived to 72, 76, 87 and 90.

The famous Joanna Baillie reached 88, and her sister Agnes 100. But the longest life belonged to a married lady, Mrs Ada Jessop (H 25), who was born in 1859 and died in 1962, aged 102–3. The higher claims of a lady, who apparently lived to 130 according to dates recorded by Millward (and now illegible), had to be treated as suspect. The mother of Norman Shaw, the architect, reached her 99th year.

Women certainly outnumbered the men in this part of the survey. Of the 96 nonagenarians recorded, 58 were female and 38 male. The men included James Pilgrim (of Pilgrim's Lane fame), who lived to 90, and George Potter, who founded the local Estate Agency, who died in 1899 aged 94. The oldest married couple were Frederick and Dorothy Daniell (A 31), who both died in 1974, aged 93. In the same grave is Frederick's sister, Elise Koch, who died in 1976 aged 97. The Rev. George Armitage and his wife, Martha (B 95), were both in their nineties.

The majority of nonagenarians are in the newer parts of the graveyard, which fact pays tribute to twentieth-century medical care, while the remarkable number of long lives recorded altogether happily preserves Hampstead's long reputation as the healthiest of London suburbs.

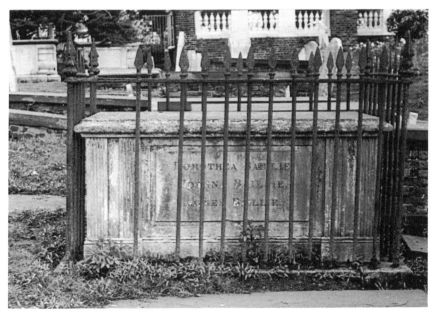

Joanna Baillie and her long-living family.

Unnatural causes

Many stories tell of the unnatural deaths of the people they commemorate – and the older the monument, the more it has to say.

In 1789, five weeks after the death of **William Chapman** of Bloomsbury, a painter ('he was a downright honest man'), his 37-year-old daughter Elizabeth 'died of a Broken Heart'. Seven years later, her 19-year-old son Peter 'fell a victim to the allurements of the ice, whilst skating on the Serpentine River' (XE 070).

The Houlditch/Snoxell tomb.

Captain Thomas Houlditch (XG 028) of His Majesty's Navy was 'lost in the East Indies 1790', while his brother Henry, a Captain in the Queen's 2nd Regiment, 'died in the West Indies of the Yellow Fever, 1795'.

In 1818, **Ellen Parry**, aged 8, 'an amiable and much lamented child, fell a victim to that cruel disease the measles, which closed thus early a life of much promise' (C 97).

The only recorded typhoid victim was **John Roberts**, LRCP, MRCS, who died in 1865 'of Typhus Fever caught in the zealous performance of his duty': he was 25 (F 61 A). The only smallpox case is mentioned on the **Gardnor** tomb (XB 011) in 1772. Both the wives of **Abraham Sibthorp** (XE 128 and 134) died in childbed, in 1724 and 1737.

The **Ambrose** family (XB 087) lost three of their sons in 1810; the eldest was 30. Lawrence died at Calcutta, Charles died at sea, and Richard was shipwrecked. Other watery graves awaited **Harry Wash** (XD 044), in 1899 'drowned in the Transvaal when rescuing a friend', **Percy Earl** (D 54), 'drowned in Torres Strait' in 1846, and the 18-year-old **Richard Mallard** (XD 185), who 'met his Fate by bathing in the Middle Pond on Hampstead Heath' in 1804. **Michael Llewelyn Davies** (J 11), 'an undergraduate, drowned at Oxford while bathing, 1921' was one of J.M. Barrie's 'Lost Boys'.

Life was no safer on dry land, even for the rich. **Sir James Mackintosh** (XB 149) died in 1832 after swallowing a chicken bone. His friend, **Thomas N. Longman** (CH 87), the prosperous publisher, was thrown from his horse on the way home from his office in 1842, and **Daniel Sharpe** (XB 136), a Portugal merchant, also had a fatal fall from his horse in 1856. **Thomas Armstrong** (G 91) 'died on Snowdon' in 1922 and **Mildred Bell** (F 10),

Longman, the publisher, who died after falling off his horse.

of another publishing family, 'died by accident on the Matterhorn' in 1901; she has edelweiss on her tombstone.

The majority of unnatural deaths, however, were victims of war. The earliest of these was **Dr William Browne** (B 2A), 'of the 95th Regt. Foot, who died at Scutari in 1854'. As this was where Florence Nightingale was operative, he may have worked in one of her hospitals, and with him may have been **Jane Pries** (XI 005), who 'died in the Crimea' in the 1850s, aged 27.

Francis Yeld (F 96), Lieut W.I.R., was surprisingly 'killed in action, Sierra Leone, 1898', two years after that colony became a protectorate. Of the two Boer War casualties, **Major Mackenzie** (D 62B) of the Seaforth Highlanders went 'missing at Magersfontein' in 1899, while **Frederick Potter** (B 26), 'Volunteer in the Imperial Light Infantry' was killed in action at Spion Kop the following year, 'aged 27 years, Faithful unto Death'.

In World War One, twenty-eight young men, mostly in their twenties, 'nobly sacrificed' their lives 'for King, Country and Humanity'. 'Dulce et decorum est,' says only one stone, 'pro patria mori.' Most were killed in action in France or Belgium, and many were buried in war cemeteries but are commemorated here. Two died at or after the Gallipoli campaign of 1915. One died 'on active service in Palestine' in 1918. Among three naval casualties, **Edward Uphill** (A 104) was a 'chaplain RN, who went down with HMS Aboukir in September 1914'. That must have been one of the first fatalities of the war, while **John McClure** (I 20), 'who died on active service, October 29, 1918' (two weeks before the Armistice), was one of the last.

Only twelve epitaphs refer to World War Two, and these are mostly in a stiff-upper-lip style. Two died on the Egyptian front in 1941–2, one at El Alamein. An Artillery Captain was killed in Italy in 1943; a corporal in the KRRC died from wounds as a prisoner of war in northern Italy in 1944, another man died as a prisoner in North Borneo in 1945. The sole air raid victim mentioned is **Joseph Gaetjens** (V 1), 'killed by enemy action, October 16th, 1940'. (This was during a week of heavy bombing, according to *Hampstead at War*, when fifty bombs fell on the borough and twenty-four people were killed.) The only other civilian casualty was the author, **Donald Carswell** (q.v.), who was 'killed in blackout accident, London' in 1940.

On a happier note, a vast number of military gentlemen seem to have survived to die in their beds. Numerous names of regiments appear in the inscriptions, which include a Colonel in the Bengal Native Cavalry (XB 180), who died in 1901; a surgeon in the Prince of Wales American Regiment (XB 054), who died in 1789; and a Guidon-Major of the 3rd Troop of Horse Guards, who died in 1740.

2. The Tombs

At least sixty-five stones were found in the survey to pre-date the present church and many more, whose dates could not be read, were presumed to be of similar antiquity. Hampstead has a particularly fine collection of Georgian limestone chest tombs, as well as many headstones that illustrate eighteenth-century symbolism. Some of the bigger chest tombs, which are shown in the engraving of the pre-1745 church, can still be seen in the churchyard. A clear example is that of Thomas Weedon, merchant, who died in 1714: his grave, on the right of the picture, is No. XB 015.

The oldest surviving stone, in the floor of the church near the north entrance, belongs to John Rixton, Gent., who was born in mid-Elizabethan times and died in 1658. His wife, Margaret, who appears to have died some thirty years later, aged 91 (the figures are not very clear), is buried with him. Their inscription, which sadly is being worn away by passing feet and a grand piano, reads:

Here under this marble is interred ye corpse of Iohn Rixton Gent., born in Great Sonky in the County of Lancaster, aged about 79 yeares, and departed this life on ye 19 day of May in ye yeare of our Lord God 1658.
And also the body of Margaret Rixton his wife, who died on the 6th day of December 1687 (?), anno salutis aged 91 (?) years.
As thou art, so was I: as I am, so shalt thou be.

A further monument to John Rixton, by the north east staircase, records his gift of £3 per annum for distribution of bread to the poor (see Appendix). His place of birth is presumably what is now called Great Sanky in Lancashire.

There are two other seventeenth-century stones in the old graveyard, the oldest (XD 109) being half buried under a path. Only the date – 1666 – is now visible, but Millward recorded the name, Elizabeth Dyer, and her age, 51 years. A little more legible is the ledger stone (XE 068) of Mr Evan Tyler, 'citizen and stationer of London', who died in 1682. Millward could read further that this tomb was erected at Mr Tyler's direction by his three executors. (Pre-1700 memorials are listed by the Royal Commission on Historic Monuments.)

Thomas Weedon

Several old tombs, recorded by past historians, have now completely disappeared. The 'faire monument of alabaster', noted by John Norden (1593) for Armigell or Armagil (DNB) Waad, was 'raised in the wall of the chancel' of the old church in 1568: the long obsequious inscription in Latin has at least survived (see Appendix). Waad and his son, Sir William, were high officials at court (see their biographies), and lived at Belsize House. This monument had gone by 1796, when Daniel Lysons surveyed the churchyard, but he did see that of Daniel Bedingfield, 'Gent. of Grays Inn, Clerk of the Parliaments', who died in 1637; he was one of an eminent East Anglian family of lawyers.

Crosses and Kerbs
The churchyard extension, with its serried ranks of crosses, kerbs and headstones, has the feel of many a Victorian cemetery, except that, now and then and here and there, it has been allowed to go wild. Many of the oldest graves are to be found at the top of the churchyard, where it was possible to have a tomb with a view – and where the drainage was better. The north east corner was a late development (1930s) and includes many ashes from cremations. This practice was legalised in 1885, but did not become widespread until World War II.

The cross, the ancient symbol of faith, is everywhere, in many varieties, from plain and concrete to Celtic and granite. Most stand on stepped plinths; some are mounted on cairns and other curious bases. Unfortunately, crosses are easily vandalised, and many here are broken or unintentionally horizontal; a few have disappeared altogether since our survey began.

The centres of some crosses have carved angels, or crucifixions, a broken lily, IHS, or Mizpah. Some are draped with stone roses (Escombe, D 59), or ivy (Lankester, D 85), or are decorated with foxes and serpents (Mort, H 6), or a life-size dove (Gow-Gregor, L 79). Angus Campbell (H 97), who won the Military Cross, has a stone shaped like the medal.

The kerb, usually marble, creeps in from the 1820s, as a tidy reminder of the grave-plot being private property. Some are filled with crazy paving or, like Anton Walbrook's (J 1), with granite chips. F 4 has a kerb of dry-stone walling, now literally dilapidated. Three kerbs incorporate bird baths; one, supported by a cherub, belongs to the mother of the actress, Gwen Ffrangcon-Davies (N 85). Kerbs have survived better at Hampstead than in many graveyards, where they have been removed to make way for the mower: this is fortunate, since they often have extra inscriptions on them.

Apart from the types of monument mentioned below, there are many shaped like open books (e.g. Ullman, Q 75), including one in a vast shell (Marten, L 82). The book – symbolising the Book of Life or the Book of Memory – became popular here from the 1920s, and seems particularly appropriate in this literate community.

Leslie Marten

Material thoughts

The majority of the oldest graves in the churchyard are of limestone, frequently Portland, or sandstone, frequently York, and have eroded badly. A few are topped with blue lias, but this has not worn well either. Three early inscriptions (1718, 1729, 1739 are on slate, however, and remain in excellent condition. Other prevalent types of stone on later tombs are marble, Yorkstone, and a variety of granites – pink, red, grey, black, polished and unpolished, Cornish and Peterhead (H. Fisher, I 95–6). There are occasional samples of Cragleith (R. Whitaker, B 19), and a few rare stones like Yugoslav Nabrazina (Collins, J 3).

Much of the metalwork on tombs has rusted away, or been removed for other reasons (wartime scrap metal, etc.). Many of the old chest tombs were originally surrounded by tall iron railings, as can still be seen intact on the tomb of Zachariah Darby (XC 003) of 1832. Railings were a valuable, if expensive, protection from passing pedestrians, from vandals, from the parson's horse or cow, which was allowed to graze in the graveyard and, in the distant past, from grave-robbers. Chest tombs themselves, and heavy ledger stones, also provided some protection, as well as showing the social superiority of the occupants. A few tombs have low, purely decorative railings, such as XB 086 (Kinder, 1864) and XB 001 (Haward, 1860): the latter has the added distinction of appearing in a *Punch* cartoon by the local artist, George du Maurier.

Zachariah Darby

"FOR THE THIRD TIME OF ASKING."

Aunt Mary. "You heard the Vicar publish the Banns between Uncle George and Ellen Thompson?"
Ethel (who has never been present at this Ceremony before). "Yes—it seems rather a Shame to tell everybody how often he's
been Refused, though!"

Du Maurier's impression of the churchyard, including the railings (left) of the Haward grave.

Body-snatching

The only known case of body-snatching at Hampstead concerned the grave of John Lloyd
(XB 199) one night in 1794, and was reported by Barratt:

> A gang of 'resurrection men' or 'body-snatchers' paid a nocturnal visit to Hampstead churchyard.
> This outrage occurred on Friday, March 14, 1794, between two and three in the morning. The
> men dug up the body of Mr John Lloyd, who had been buried the day before, put it into a sack, and
> conveyed it to a hackney coach in waiting to receive it, but the local watchman pounced upon them,
> stopped the coach, and with assistance arrested two men found inside, who gave the names of Tom
> Paine and Peter Mackintosh. . . . The corpse and the men's shovels, tools, etc., for opening the
> coffin were taken possession of, and the prisoners and the coachman were 'carried before Master
> Montagu and committed to gaol'. Two others of the party made their escape, 'one of whom had the
> appearance of a gentleman', and was supposed to be a surgeon.

Master Montagu was a Master in Chancery, living in the upper part of Frognal, known as
Montagu Grove.

Pride of place

Tradition has it that, in most churchyards, the elite are buried on the south side of the
church, and the north is reserved for beggars and others who cannot be choosers –
suicides, paupers and unbaptised infants. This latter superstition – that the north was 'the
devil's side' – was not evidenced in our survey, but the southern side of the church

William Taylor

certainly was closer packed and full of the high and mighty. At the same time, they were not mighty enough to have themselves buried inside the church, which was much to be desired.

One who had such ambitions was William Taylor, Esq., whose crumbling monument (XE 001) is on the south-east exterior wall of the church. The inscription, quoted in full by Park, tells the whole sad story, that he was 'several years one of the pages of the bed-chamber to their Majesties King George the First and Second; was always a careful, diligent, and faithful servant. He died the 12th of June 1747, aged 63. By his will he left several annuities and legacies to his relations, servants, and to the poor, and others; and in his life-time gave fifty pounds towards the rebuilding of this church, and earnestly desired to be interred therein, but after his decease, although the utmost solicitations were made use of by his executors, that favour could not be obtained for his remains.' What had he done to deserve this? One can only wonder if perhaps he died too soon. At the time of his death, the new church was not quite ready and, until it was consecrated on October 8, 1747, nobody could be buried inside its unhallowed walls.

The vast majority of headstones face east, that is with the main inscription on the eastern side. The Christian custom of burying corpses on their backs on an east-west alignment, and facing east, allowed them when the Resurrection dawned to sit up and see it immediately before them.

Skulls and crossbones
Hampstead has a fine collection of memorials showing the Georgian love of symbolism.

George Russell

Christopher Walker

'The imagery on post-Reformation monuments,' says Burgess, 'is mainly concerned with the expression of the three themes of Mortality, Resurrection and the Means of Salvation.' We have good examples of all of these, especially on the grave of Gillam Scott (XB 142), which has more than most. Others are noted below in the Good Grave Guide.

The skull and crossed bones were the most popular symbol, because they not only signified the inevitability of Death, but hinted at the possibility of Resurrection. The bones were supposed to be thighbones as, technically, the basic equipment for rising from the tomb was believed to be a skull and two such bones.

The hourglass was another symbol for Death, which is seen on several tombs (e.g. Russell, XE 012), sometimes with wings (e.g. Gillam Scott, XB 142), to show how time flies. Towards the end of the Georgian period, a frequent motif for mortality was the urn, of which we have many versions inside the church. The urn harked back vaguely to the funerary urns of pre-Roman times but, more relevantly, was popularised by the Greek revival of the Adam brothers. Resurrection was also symbolised by the cherub's head (e.g. XI 029), representing the metamorphosis of the soul.

Means of Salvation were shown by such allegorical figures as Faith, Hope and Charity. Faith has as her sign the ubiquitous cross, which is much in evidence in the 1812 churchyard. Hope with her anchor, and Charity with her heart, are beautifully sculpted on the monument to Lord Erskine's wife (CH 77) in the church.

Such imagery gradually disappeared in the nineteenth century, as the work of craftsmen was usurped by the mass production of tombstones to meet an ever-increasing demand.

Symbols on stones

anchor	hope
angel's head	resurrection
cross	faith/victory over death
dove	Holy Spirit
flambeau	life
heart	charity
hourglass	time passing
ivy	everlasting life
lily	purity
palms	victory
rose	virtue
skull and crossbones	death/resurrection
trumpets	triumph
urn	mortality

More stones with symbols

XB 185 skull, 1781 (Christopher Walker)

XD 012 skull & crossbones, 1730 (Elizabeth Billson)

XD 032 angel's head, no date (Elizabeth Miller)

XD 047 skull, hourglass, 1720 (Jane Bleake)

XD 054 skull & crossbones, 1728 (Sarah Knight)

XD 072 open book and foliage, 1763 (James Pitt)

XD 111 angel and foliage, 1770 (William Birch)

XD 118 angel and foliage, 1770 (Susannah Wear)

XE 121 skull & crossbones, 1739 (Thomas Hull)

XE 127 skull & crossbones, 1773 (Alice Goffe)

XE 133 skull & crossbones, 1753 (Abraham Sibthorp)

XE 141 skull & crossbones, 1732 (Mary Buckeridge)

XF 036 skull, scrolls, trumpets, 1721 (Margaret Clarke)

XI 029 angels' heads, trumpets, 1763 (Ann Powell)

Gillam Scott

Margaret Clarke

3. The Inscriptions

'The epitaph,' writes Kenneth Lindley in *Of Graves and Epitaphs*, 'is one of the richest and yet most neglected sources of information on the lives and customs of our ancestors . . . and an interesting introduction to social history.'

Both the prose and the poetry on our gravestones, much of it in a sorry style and sentiment, reflect the varying social and religious attitudes of our earlier communities. Unfortunately, many of the epitaphs quoted below are now practically illegible, or only visible in certain lights. Some of the verses quoted may well be found in other graveyards, as they were often lifted from standard collections of epitaphs supplied by stonemasons.

Praise indeed

A curious old custom, seen on many of our Georgian tombstones, was the eulogy. 'To speak with justice,' says one inscription[24], 'her true character would appear like flattery.' Many a lady is said to have had 'manners most unblamable'[25]; a mother is called 'a most careful and discreetly indulgent parent'[26], and a wife is lauded to the skies because her 'understanding, knowledge, talents, piety, benevolence and every active and exemplary Christian virtue made her the object of love and esteem throughout her whole life'[27]. The housekeeper for 56 years with the Merry family, who is buried next to them, receives her tribute in verse[28]:

Amongst those silent mansions of the dead
A valiant old domestic rests her head . . .
At duty's call, she cheerfully obeyed
And strict fidelity and truth displayed . . . (and 8 more such lines)

Some of the praise is cautiously qualified: 'She had many very good qualities which, if she had any faults – and there are few which have none – it is hoped were sufficient to atone for them.' (XD 022, Sophia Willes)

Gentlemen are commended mainly for not losing their tempers. A Russian merchant[29] was 'highly respected for the singular mildness of his manner', and James Pilgrim, the local landowner, who lived to be 90, was noted for his 'inflexible integrity, unaffected humility, true benevolence and placidity of temper' (XB 178).

Honesty was also the policy of John Holton Vere (C 6), who is saluted in some blunt and misspelt couplets:

Here lies an odd but honest man,
Reader, deny it if you can!
His promise shure nor word would break,
Though by it might a fortune make;
Gold and silver not his pride,
From honors, fame, he'd step aside;
Ye learned, noble, haughty great,
Persue and read – go imitate!

Two other eighteenth century worthies have the same epigram[30,31]:

This modest stone – what few vain marbles can –
May truly say Here Lies An Honest Man.

An upholsterer of Heath Street (XF 064) was rather ambiguously 'respected and regretted by all who knew him', while William Usherwood of Kilburn Wells (CH 23) advised, 'What you have seen amiss in me, mend in yourselves!'

The same defiant attitude was shown by a lady of 51 – and possibly of easy virtue – (C 4), who seemed to welcome her death in 1822[32]:

> Farewell, vain world! I've had enough of thee,
> And careless ever what thou sayest of me,
> Thy smiles I court not, nor thy frowns I fear;
> Blessed by the Lord, my head lies (happy) here.
> The faults you've seen in me, take care to shun!
> And look at home – there's something to be done.

Attitudes to Death

A strong sense of realism and resignation pervades the epitaphs of Georgian times. 'In this vault lies, in hope of a joyful resurrection, the mortal part of Mr John Tean,' says XB 218. 'Reader, emulate his virtues and do all the good you can.' Mr Tean was a vice-president of the philanthropic Philo-Investigists in 1787 (see p. 48). The inscription for an eight-year-old girl[33] concludes: 'It has pleased the Almighty to call her from this Vale of Tears to the Mansions of Bliss. We must therefore, in dutiful resignation to His will, cease to mourn her loss.' Many a verse shows parents bowing to the inevitable loss of their infants – for instance, on six-week-old William Arthur Chamberlayne in 1815:

> An infant dear lies sleeping here
>   To keep us fresh in mind
> That die we must, be turned to dust,
>   And leave this world behind. (B 23)

and on two-year-old Maria Essex in 1793:

> Happy the babe, so privileged by fate
> To shorter labour and a lighter weight. (XB 106)

The most frequently found verse, first seen here in the 1750s, is[34]:

> Afflictions sore long time I bore,
>   Physicians were in vain,
> Till God did please to give me ease
>   And free me from my pain.

This jingle is found, with variations, in many parts of the country, and was still being used in our churchyard in the 1880s.

Other deaths evidently came suddenly – for instance, to the 56-year-old wife of Charles Barton of the Inner Temple (XE 043) in 1821:

> At morn in cheerful Health she rose, at noon and eve the same,
> At night retired to calm repose, the awful Summons came;
> Think then how soon thy time may come
> To rest within the dreary Tomb,
> And hold prepared, if snatched away,
> The Instant Summons to obey!

Several poems preach an urgent message of repentance to the reader, such as this in 1822[35]:

> Weep not for me, 'tis all in vain –
> Weep for your sins, from them refrain!

and this in 1806[36]:

> Go home, dear friends, dry up your tears,
> I might be here till Christ appears;
> My debt is paid, my grave you see,
> Prepare yourselves to follow me!

Charles and Fanny Lord

The apocryphal answer to this was scrawled in another churchyard:
> To follow you is my intent,
> But no one knows which way you went.

A further exhortation against mourning was attributed to a young wife in 1826[37]:
> Farewell, my husband and three children dear,
> Grieve not for me though I lay buried here . . .

The husband evidently obeyed, as he buried his second wife here three years later.

Victorian values

The influence of the High Church movement of the 1840s is clearly visible in the later epitaphs: 'There is no death. What seems so is transition.'[38] Death, said the pundits, was a pagan concept full of despair, and gravestones should proclaim the victory of the dear departed. 'There is an angel which opens the prison door,' says D 76 (Fanny Lord), 'We wrong him when we call him Death.'[39] St Paul was quoted as an authority, as he referred to his demise as a 'departure'. Other Biblical evidence was found, including St Stephen, who merely 'fell asleep'. The epitaph writers coined many a euphemism for death, stressing the comforts of being carried home to an endless rest. More and more graves wore a cross as a symbol of triumph over death. Many philosophically quoted the Book of Job: 'The Lord giveth and the Lord taketh away. Blessed be the name of the Lord.'[40] The next world was made to sound highly desirable. 'With Christ, which is far better' is a frequent Biblical quotation[41], and 'To die is to gain'.[42]

Those who died young were much envied:
> Happy child, thy warfare's ended,
> Now the glorious prize hast won . . .[43]

and
> Oh happy dead, your quiet bed
>   With tearful hope I view,
> Welcome the day when I shall lay
>   My weary head with you.[44]

The simplicity and tranquillity of death was also emphasised. 'Her end was peace' was applied to many an old lady,[45] without saying who found peace, the dead or the living; and of Mr William Negus, of the Green Man, Finchley, Licensed Victualler (XG 022), it was noted that 'he died without a murmur'.

Eulogies were now discouraged. 'Their fulsomeness and utter want of truth,' wrote a nineteenth-century cleric, 'outdo anything of that kind in the pagan world itself, so that "to lie like an epitaph" has grown into a saying.'

A rather mean stone of 1849 states:
> Praises on tombs are trifles vainly spent;
> A man's good life is his best monument.[46]

However, a young vicar received this tribute in 1851:
> His dear memory will ever be cherished in the hearts of those to whom his engaging talents and sweetness of character cannot die any more . . .[47]

And of the great preacher, Stopford Brooke (J 30), it was said in 1916: 'His word was a kindling fire, giving strength to the weak . . . and wings to the strong.'

William Negus, the publican, who 'died without a murmur'.

Love and Joy

From the 1920s, there is a growing emphasis on love – for instance, 'Love is stronger than Death'[48] 'To live in hearts we leave behind is not to die' (Campbell) is quoted on Harry Holmes (C 42). 'Life that is love is God' is the comment on Eva Gore-Booth (B 27). 'We loved her, yes we loved her, but Jesus loved her more'[49] is presumably from a Mission Hall hymn. A local policeman in 1935 is said to have been:

Loving and kind in all his ways,
Upright and just to the end of his days.[50]

Not all married couples had a life of bliss. A wife comments on a husband[51] that he was 'light and shadow by turns', and a husband unkindly remembered his wife with Luke, Chapter VII: 'Her sins, which are many, are forgiven.'

Flowers and gardens flourish in the epitaphs of the thirties and forties. A dead daughter is described as 'our beautiful flower, transplanted to God's garden'[52] and 'life is a forecourt, death a gate: the beyond of both a garden'.[53]

An architect, who died in 1964, has this on his well-planted grave:

Death cannot long divide,
For is it not as though
The rose that climbed my garden wall
Had blossomed on the other side?
Death doth hide but not divide;
Thou art but on Christ's other side. (Albert John Packe Thomas, J 36)

Cheerfulness breaks through in the later twentieth century. 'Because of you we will be glad and gay',[54] and 'He cheered the sad and the happy he made happier'.[55] Merriest of all is the 1954 epitaph of the limerick writer and editor, Langford Reed (D 35) – author unknown:

There once was a fellow named Reed,
Who knew that the world had a need
  For Limericks and fun,
  And all hearts he won,
Since laughter and joy were his creed.

The laughter and joy will not die,
As angels laugh with him on high,
  While we here on earth
  Should cultivate mirth;
'Tis better to laugh than to cry.

A 1965 stone says, 'Sing upon the high hills',[56] and a 1977 inscription to a father and mother ends, 'Heaven give you many, many, merry days'. As the same stone comments, 'Remember there is no tragedy in death, except to the living.'[57] In recent years, expression of sentiment and praise, as well as exuberance in the design of monuments, has sadly been discouraged by the Church. As their *Churchyards Handbook* of 1962 says: 'The main object of the inscription is not to commemorate the dead person, but to indicate the place of his burial.'

Original design for tomb of Nathaniel Booth, Lord Delamer.

More epitaphs

Infants

1814
Here sleeps a babe whose lively charms
    Did oft her parents' hearts allure,
Fondly they pressed her in their arms,
    And hoped those charms would long endure;
But He whose power first gave her breath,
    Observing she their idol grew,
Soon summoned her to quit the earth,
    And up to Him her spirit flew.
(Caroline Pothonier, B 84–7)

1857
Brief was his span of life, sweet now his rest;
He left no trace behind, save in a parent's breast.
(Christian Hamilton, XB 228)

Husbands and Wives

1756
Her life was an amiable triumph of conjugal virtue,
accompanied with a resignation becoming a good
and faithful servant. (Susannah Godfrey, XB 167)

1820
No tongue can tell the precious loss,
    Or anguish of the mind,
But her who bears this heavy cross,
    His widow, left behind.
(James Budd, XE 064)

1854
Dearest friends, as you pass by,
Remember in the dust you must lie;
These worldly gains you must leave behind,
And, perhaps like me, be cut off in your prime.
(Elizabeth Green, XI 010)

Sons and Daughters

1757
Rest undisturb'd ye much lamented pair
The smiling infant and the rising Heir,
Ah! what avails it that the blossoms shoot
In early Promise of maturer Fruit,
If Death's chill Hand shall nip their Infant Bloom,
And wither all their Honours in the Tomb!
Yet weep not if, in Life's allotted Share,
Swift fled their Youth – they knew not Age's Care.
(Lord Delamer's children, XD 092)

1765
Heav'nward directed all her days,
Her life one act of prayer and praise,
With every milder grace inspir'd,
To make her lov'd, esteem'd, admir'd:
Crown'd with a cheerfulness that show'd
How pure the source from whence it flow'd:
Such was the maid – when in her bloom,
Finding th'appointed time was come,
To sleep she sunk, without one sigh –
The saint may sleep, but cannot die.
(Hon. Elizabeth Booth, XD 092)

1768
In Bloom of years a maiden here doth lie,
Then drop a tear in gentle sympathy,
And think how soon the fairest flower must die.
(Mary Bell, XB 038)

1823
Her parents perform the untimely duty of bearing
witness on this tablet that bodily sufferings long
endured, in the natural season of gladness, were so
alleviated by a meek Spirit and a humble Piety that
they neither interrupted the cultivation of her
Understanding, nor obscured her native
Gracefulness, but rather seemed to place in a softer
light the delicate Propriety, which was the ornament
of her spotless Life, and to prepare her gentle virtues
for a State more congenial to them. (Elizabeth
Mackintosh, CH 7)

1833
All cheering Spring had rear'd the Bud,
Sweet Summer spread the Bloom,
Scarce Matron Autumn's part commenced
Ere Winter sealed its doom.
(Jane Robinson, G 40)

1864
A Mother dear, a Wife sincere,
A loving Friend lies buried here;
Our loss is great, we'll not complain,
But trust in Christ to meet again.
(Maria Watts, XG 010)

1874
Soft hiv'd with wing and plume
Thou in his shroud shalt lie.
This stone is set up by her husband, her children
and her brother, who live in daily thought of her,
who of herself took no thought . . . (Emma Brooke,
J 30)

Repent!

1837
In peace I lay me down to rest,
The Lord of Life has conquered Death;
From sin and guilt has set me free –
I hope he'll do the same for thee.
(Negus family, XG 022)

1846
Hear now this preaching grave without delay!
Believe, repent, and work, while yet 'tis day!
Make every day a critique on the past,
And live each hour, as if it were your last!
(William Francis, B 67)

General

1803
(On a cosmopolitan lady, daughter of Henry and
Justina Davidson of Tulloch, XB 202)
Italia matrem dedit huic, Caledonia patrem,
Nascente Africa solum renascente Anglia,
Virginis quae tam teneris annis
Terram caelo mutans, parentes et aulam Deo,
Nunc pro fratre sororibusque angelos complectitur.
(Freely translated)
Her mother was Italian, her father was a Scot,
Though she was born in Africa, in England was her lot;
She left her home and parents for Heaven's exalted
charms,
Exchanged her brother, sisters, all, for angels' loving
arms.

1864
Farewell! We did not know thy worth,
But thou art gone and now 'tis prized;
So angels walked unknown on earth,
And when they flew were recognised.
(William Harris, B 16)

1851
Weep not for me, my parent dear,
I am not dead, but sleeping here,
My end you know, my grave you see,
Therefore prepare to follow me.
(Alfred Love, XD 010)

1944
Do not ask us if we miss him,
   There is such a vacant place,
Could we ere forget his footsteps,
   Or his dearly smiling face?
(George Day, C 33)

1871
Faithfull (*sic*) friends and parents dear,
A tender Father, Mother, Aunt sleepeth here,
Who laboured hard with toil and care
With a reward from God to share.
(Hayter family, G 48)

1875
We all like forest trees do stand,
   Some are doomed to fall,
We all must go at God's command,
   And thus obey his call.
(Knapp family, XD 134)

Graves mentioned in this section

	Grave No.	Name			Grave No.	Name
1	XD 029	John Hollister		30	XB 150	David Middleton
2	CR 14	Thomas Phill		31	XG 016	John Eades
3	XH 004	James Roades		32	C 4	Ann Glaisher
4	XE 121	Thomas Hull		33	C 97	Ellen Parry
5	XH 005	William Barry		34	XB 142	Thomas Scott
6	XE 014A	William Smith		35	XD 036	Morris Lincoln
7	XD 161	Thomas Rayer		36	XG 004	James Bill
8	XE 157	John Williamson		37	E 49–50	Sarah Gamble
9	XE 147	Thomas Humphrey		38	C 77	Charles Henry Hill
10	XD 128	Alexander Palmer		39	D 76	Fanny Lord
11	XB 139	Samuel Cossens		40	XE 022	Hope family
12	XB 140	Edward Helling		41	E 27	Susannah Burt
13	XD 110	John Smith		42	D 105	Mary Moor
14	CR 3	George Hill		43	XG 025	John Peacock
15	XH 029	Joseph Affleck		44	XH 036	James Francis
16	XL 015	Thomas Allport		45	XG 022	Negus family
17	XD 141	John Hanson		46	XD 037	James Starkey
18	XD 155	Richard Wiggins		47	XB 227	William Porter
19	XF 037	Charles Ellis		48	N 65	Margaret Galloway
20	XK 001	Thomas Clark		49	G 23	Mary Jane Adams
21	CH 51	William Wood		50	M 72	Richard Steers
22	XD 015	Edward Adams		51	D 88	Rosalind Saunders
23	XD 149	H.W. Mortimer		52	L 65	H.M. Siewert
24	C 24–7	Hannah Virgin		53	N 101	S.F. Jell
25	XE 089	Margaret Ouchterlony		54	I 78	Olivia Davidson
26	XD 092	Lady Delamer		55	I 92	Neil Fell-Clark
27	XB 141	Marianne Mathias		56	H 105	Amelia Robinson
28	XD 008	Eleanor Meredith		57	G 67	Evelyn Green
29	XB 174	Cornwall Smalley				

IV GOOD GRAVE GUIDE

Hampstead churchyard has many graves of interest, some because of their style or symbolism, others because of their occupants. This section covers the monuments themselves, with particular reference to their design and decoration. In many cases, there is further biographical detail in the next section.

Tombs are listed here, starting with the old graveyard, in order of reference numbers: the numbering system is explained on page 11. The graves can roughly be located from the map at the back of this book, or pinpointed from the large-scale maps in the church and at the Local History Library at Swiss Cottage.

Quotations are taken from the monumental inscriptions unless another source is given.

1. Old Churchyard

XB 003: **Thomas Hood**, 'late of Grays Inn, Gentleman', who died 1754, has a handsome pedestal tomb, but has lost his headpiece, which was presumably an urn: fortunately his coat-of-arms is still clear. In the same grave are a mason of Lincolns Inn Fields, and an eminent Land Surveyor of Little Missenden, Bucks.

XB 011: **Thomas Gardnor's** tomb (1775), near the main gate, is one of the finest in the churchyard: a decorated limestone base supports a sculptured pedestal and urn. There is a coat-of-arms and beautiful cursive flourishes in the inscription. The whole was restored in 1982 in memory of Charles Mallord Turner, a former churchwarden. Gardnor owned much property in Hampstead, and built Gardnor House in Gardnor Road in 1736.

XB 015: **Thomas Weedon** (died 1714), a local merchant, has an unusual limestone chest tomb, with curved top and ends (see page 28).

XB 128: The family of **Norman Shaw**, RA, champion of the Queen Anne revivial, has a Georgian-style limestone chest tomb, designed by Ernest Newton and Laurence Turner in 1913, the year after the architect's death. The ends and sides are swagged with wings, tassels and foliage.

XB 141: **William Popple** (died 1722), Secretary to the Board of Trade, has a chest tomb in Greek Revival style, erected (over an older vault) by his granddaughter in c. 1782. The top curves up to a pedestal, but the urn (?) is missing.

The Gardnor tomb

XB 142: **Gillam Scott**, who was the son of a 'mason

and citizen of London', and died very young in 1735, has 3 cherub heads and some rosettes on one side, and skull and crossbones and a winged hour-glass on the other.

XB 158: **Rev. James Burn** (died 1794), 'many years senior chaplain to the Presidency of Calcutta', has an elaborately carved sarcophagus with a scrolled top and crests at each end.

XB 161: **James Jowitt** (1775) is an example of the twin-panel tombstone – a line drawn down the middle allows for two parallel inscriptions. In this case one panel was never filled, while on XH 012 (1781), the **Wildman** sisters are given equal importance in the duplex design.

XB 202: The **Davidson** chest tomb of c. 1800 has a particularly fine crest on the south side – two cartouches, flanked by griffins and surmounted by a winged crown. The main inscription is in Latin (see p. 44).

XB 223: **Rev. Thomas Ainger** (1799–1863), 'XXII years incumbent of this parish', has a highly decorated tomb, surrounded by ornamental railings. The tomb itself is in the shape of a bodystone, with a Bible and chalice incised on either side of an elaborate horizontal cross, and with Gothic lettering round the edge.

Rev. Thomas Ainger

XC 002: **John Constable** has a classical limestone chest tomb, surrounded by tall railings. The monument, dating from the death of his wife in 1828, was restored by public subscription during the bicentenary celebrations of 1976. There was not enough money to do this in his daughter Isabella's bequest of £50 'to keep the family vault in good repair . . . any surplus to be given to relieving the poor and respectable inhabitants of Hampstead'. (Picture on page 7)

XC 006: **John Hodgson**, who died in 1858, has an artistic memorial in Portland stone, including scrolls, angels and a winged cherub's head.

John Hodgson

XC 007: The **Purton** tomb (1841) has a decorated gothic arcade, surrounded by railings, with a gate. William Purton was one of Constable's closest Hampstead friends.

XD 009: **Captain John Merry** (died 1728), 'many years a Governor of the Hudson Bay Company', has a fine Portland chest tomb, enriched with a crest. Adjoining headstones have affectionate epitaphs for two of his servants.

XD 019: see page 27, **Dyer**.

XD 041: **Elizabeth Cole** (died 1749) has a worn sculpture of the Eye of the Lord, a resurrection scene, and possibly a dog in the left corner.

XD 092: The chest tomb of **Nathaniel Booth**, Lord Delamer (died 1770), has elaborate swags on the sides, lions at north and south ends, and eagles on the east and west. The podium on top has lost its urn, but see picture of original design, p. 43.

XD 190: **Thomas Mitchell** (died 1799), local schoolmaster, has three inter-linked triangles on his

William Purton

headstone, signifying that he was a member of the Hampstead Philo-Investigists. This curiously-named club loved investigating all subjects of educational value to the local community. Their good works included setting up Hampstead's first Sunday school, which was the origin of the present Hampstead Parochial School in Hollybush Vale.

XD 200: The 1864 brick vault of **Basil Woodd**, 'father of the London wine trade', is topped by a squat chest tomb of pink granite, with mini-pillars at the corners and white marble slabs on the sides.

XE 001: see page 32, **Taylor**.

XE 007: **John Harrison**, 'the Man who discovered Longitude', who died in 1776, has a Portland chest tomb, decorated with pilasters and rosettes in Adam style. The lengthy inscriptions (see Appendix) are on marble plaques on the sides. According to further inscriptions, the tomb was 'reconstructed at the expense of the Worshipful Company of Clockmakers of the City of London 1879', and 'renewed and railings removed 1934'. (Pictures on pages 16 and 86)

Thomas Mitchell's headstone, showing the Philo-Investigist symbol.

XE 009: **Stephen Guyon** (died 1779), of a family of Huguenot origin, has a limestone chest tomb with a coped top. (Picture on page 17)

XE 012: '**Mr George Russell**, farrier, late of this parish', who died in 1769, has a scrolled cartouche with a cherub's head, hour glass, bones and open book.

XE 015A: **Mr Thomas Hayes**, surgeon, died in 1787, aged 36. The familiar eulogy, which begins 'a man of real merit, blessed with native talents, emulous, diligent . . .' is perhaps mercifully cut short by erosion. The triangles on his headstone show that he was a Hampstead Philo-Investigist (see above – XD 190).

XE 036: **Mr Francis Pain**, 'Cornchandler and Citizen of London', who died in 1750, has two skulls on his (now flattened) headstone.

XE 040: **Robert Atkinson** of Lincolns Inn, Gentleman, died in 1748. He is buried with his sister, **Tabitha Hutchinson**, of Staindrop in the County of Durham. Theirs is an elaborate limestone chest tomb, with a blue lias top, including a family crest.

XE 056: **Mr Edward Lucas**, butcher of this parish,

who died in 1744, has an hourglass and skull on his horizontal headstone.

XE 061: **William Hart**, 'late Citizen and Salter of London', who died in 1717, is buried with his son, John, 'Citizen and Mercer of London', and **Robert Cary, Esq.** (presumably a son-in-law), in the most elaborate chest tomb in the churchyard. Perhaps to make up for the absence of any crest, there are swags and tassels and ribbons, skulls and crossbones and cherubs' heads. The main inscription on top can be read only in certain lights when the sun is low, or at dusk with the aid of a torch: that on the south side, to **Miss Amy Cary**, who died in 1756, aged 17, 'universally lamented', can be seen to be calligraphically elegant. This tomb gave rise to the notorious Tiramiet puzzle (see p. 15).

Detail from the Hart/Carey tomb (see also p. 84).

XE 062: **Lady Elizabeth Norton**, daughter of the Earl of Gainsborough, who died in 1715, has an attractive table tomb with six arcaded legs. The inscription emphasises her humility, which made her choose to be buried most condescendingly in Hampstead.

XE 068: see page 27, **Tyler**.

Lady Elizabeth Norton

XE 117: **Jonathan Key, Esq.**, the wholesale stationer, who died in 1805, has a family tomb almost identical with that of John Harrison – but often submerged in ivy.

XE 158: **Wallis** (1779) and XE 161 (**Dennett** 1812) both appear to be ledger stones, but were once altar tombs with brick sides. The bricks had become so damaged in recent years that they were removed and the capstone lowered to the ground.

XF 011: The plain chest tomb of **Philip Fenton** (died 1806), of Fenton House, has old limestone sides, but a new composition slab on top: the lettering on the top is presumably a facsimile of old writing.

XF 032: **Thomas Packer**, who died in 1733, has a fine collection of symbols – skull and crossbones, trumpets, lilies and palms.

XG 028: The **Snoxell** (1748) and **Houlditch** (1790) tomb is a curious amalgam of styles – a brick altar tomb with portland top, base and plaques. The Snoxells were farmers and pub-owners; the Houlditches were minor gentry or military. Were the two family graves joined together when they were moved from the crypt room site in 1912? (Picture on page 25)

XH 012: see XB 161.

2. 1812 Churchyard Extension

A 17: **William Bird** (1887) is a good example of the solid, respectable grave – a mound of red, polished Peterhead granite, with posts and metal chains. Bird was one of the first inhabitants of the new Fitzjohns Avenue, in a house called Grosvenor Lodge (No. 18). See also C 94, **Parshall** (1910), with its heavy slabs of pink Aberdeen granite.

A 28: **Alexander Koch** (1911), an architect from Zurich, has an unusual podium monument.

A 35: **Elizabeth Rundle Charles** (1896), a popular Victorian writer, has an elaborate wheelcross, covered in hieroglyphics.

A 54: **Francis Ball** (1844) has one of the few chest tombs in the new graveyard, but it is tapered and decorated in different fashion from the eighteenth-century variety. K 62 (1867), the tomb of **James Smith**, is very similar.

Francis Ball

A 66: **Eve Hammersley** (1902) is an outstanding shrine-tomb for the young daughter of a family who lived at Admiral's House. The limestone shrine is on a tall pedestal and contains a bronze statue of a winged youth, cradling a sleeping girl in his arms; this is signed by Harry Furse, who exhibited at the Royal Academy between 1891 and 1909.

Eve Hammersley

A 95: **Vernon Selley** (1909) has an unusually craggy and chunky headstone, decorated with lilies and roses. The mason was J. Joslin of East Finchley.

B 10: **Paul Addison** (1912) has a 'deadboard', a horizontal wooden board, supported by upright posts: this was one of the earliest types of memorial known, and also called a grave rail or bed head, but most pre-1800 examples have rotted away. This board has copper capping and shows some influence from the Arts and Crafts movement. Note also C 22

Eva Gore-Booth

C 29: **Maria Tyson** (1828) has one of the few draped urns in this part of the graveyard – in this case, on a tall pedestal. D 76 **Lord** (1872) is of almost identical design (see page 39). J 10 (1921) has an undraped urn for **Sir John Hare**.

C 88: **George Tunley** (1897) has one of the graveyard's few obelisks – in this case, about 11 feet high. It is topped by a cross which, as Burgess suggests, is to disguise its pagan character. The obelisk has no relevance to Christianity, but became popular from 1878, when Cleopatra's Needle was set up on the Embankment. An earlier obelisk is found at F 74 (**Wilkinson** 1856) and a later one at J 14 (**Hickey** 1921).

C 94: see A 17.

C 104: **Soldiers' Daughters** (1902–41) is one of several mass graves in the 1812 extension for girls from local Homes (originally orphanages started after the Crimean War). The inscriptions, which include the regiments of the daughters' fathers, have survived very well on the enormous slate slabs. See F 85 for an earlier (1856) and prettier monument to Soldiers' Daughters, and F 16 and G 15 for Sailors' Orphan Girls.

(1908), E 31 (**Shattock** 1909), the damaged F 95 (**Chandler** 1915), and the du Maurier grave, I Bay (see below).

B 27: **Eva Gore-Booth** (1926) has a headstone of Corsham stone (yellow sandstone). On this is a cross and relief lettering in Lombardic style.

B 57: **Catherine Taylor** (1933) has an elegantly carved headstone, with cherub and foliage, possibly the work of her husband, L. Campbell Taylor, RA.

B 85: **George Gilbert Scott** (1897), architect son of the great Scott, has a horizontal hipped slab of Portland stone, with a carved cross, on a grey granite base.

B 87: **Ernest Tidey** (1865) has a panel inset on his headstone, showing a hand, surrounded by clouds. This is now very worn but the hand probably had a pointing finger, like a medieval Divine Hand.

C 22: **E.B. Stamp** (1908), the High Street chemist, has a deadboard (see B 10) but in marble, not wood.

Soldiers' Daughters

D Bay 3: **Mary Macirone** (1879) is a charming example of the duplex headstone, with parallel inscriptions, a central crest and two crosses fleury; the lettering is incised Gothic.

D 76: see C 29.

D 88: **Rosalind Saunders** (1929) is one of several mock rock-gardens, here seen with a model lamb on its kerb. M 69 (**Alfred Johnson** 1958) is a miniature landscaped garden, with steps and sundial, and M 83 (**Amy Mount** 1936), the most detailed, has a bench and paths and a sundial, which has sadly lost its head.

Amy Mount's landscaped garden.

E Bay 1: **Charles Bean King** (1928), of the local building firm, has an unexpectedly grandiose chest tomb (one of the few in the extension), very similar in design to the eighteenth-century examples in the old graveyard.

E 5: **George Gray** (1881) is an attractive horizontal slab, with a fleury cross (Mason: Daniels of Highgate). This grave was originally in the old churchyard in Plot XH but, like G 49 **Edney** (1881), was at some time moved across the road.

E 12: **Michael Ming** (1829) has not only a headstone and matching footstone, but a horizontal bodystone linking the two. K 78 (**Stout** 1831) is similar. The bodystone was a very early (seventeenth-century) protective feature of graves, which returned to favour with the Gothic Revival. A popular variation was the coped ledger stone, e.g. F 21 (**Kennerley** 1873), sometimes with a cross on the ridge, e.g. E 77 (**Burlison** 1868).

E 21: **Walter Hall** (1908) has his inscription on an ambitious marble scroll propped up on the grave. Scrolls on other graves are mostly much smaller, e.g. E 35 (**Freeman** 1929).

E 31: see B 10.

E 35: see E 21.

E 77: see E 12.

E 85: **Edwin Lankester** (1874), Coroner for Central Middlesex, has heavy chains on corner posts around his grave, when railings were no longer in fashion. Few chains have survived *in toto*.

F Bay 1: **T.F. Tout** (1929), the eminent historian, has an original variation on the bodystone in Corsham stone.

F 16: see C 104.

F 21: see E 12.

F 74: see C 88.

F 85: see C 104.

F 95: see B 10.

F 101: **Geoffrey Gilbert Scott** (1919) has a square portland urn, lead-lined to take plants. The style is classical, with rosettes and palmettes on all sides.

Thomas Tout

Sir Herbert Beerbohm Tree

Kay Kendall (Harrison)

G Bay: **Beerbohm Tree** (1917), the great actor manager, has a 6 ft. statue of a mourning maiden standing on a 2 ft. plinth. Whatever the material – probably composition – it has crumbled badly.

G 12: **Mary Martelli** (1916) is a wooden cross, with a triangular top, reminiscent of alpine wayside memorials. M 80 (1935) for **Basil Champneys** is similar in shape, but of grey granite and including Christ crucified.

G 15: see C 104.

G 49: see E 5.

H 4: **Kay Kendall** (1959), the actress, has a striking headstone of green Westmoreland slate, with large letters and squirls, designed by Reynolds Stone (1909–79).

H 6: **George Mort** (1918), pioneer of aeroplane engines, has a handsome Celtic cross, decorated with foxes and serpents and bosses. The same family has a similar cross, I 7 (1924), with even more decoration, writhing with snakes, human shapes and mythical beasts.

H 18: **Emily Nesbitt** (1918) has a curious, heavy granite headstone, shaped like a Cornish cross with a sturdy crucifixion on the reverse.

H 20: **Matthew Maris** (1917), the artist, has a low walled enclosure of concrete, decorated with sculpted crosses and bunches of grapes.

H 57: **Donald Baylis** (1920) has lost his ten-foot cross, photographed for this survey in 1976, but has kept his minute stone harp at the base.

H 77: **Herbert Pawling** (1923) has a temple-shaped stele, featuring a shield, palms and crossed flambeaux.

H 97: **Angus Campbell** (1919), MC, Royal Engineers, has a granite headstone in the shape of a Military Cross. Like that cross, it has crowns at each tip and a central monogram, GRI (Georgius Rex Imperator = George V).

I Bay: **George du Maurier** (1896), cartoonist and novelist, has the oldest of the deadboards in the churchyard. Like B 10 above, it has artistic copper capping, but here the board is supported at each end by a Celtic cross of wood. (Picture on page 10).

Hugh Gaitskell

The grave of Donald Baylis (H 57), photographed for this survey in 1976, has now lost its ten-foot cross but kept its minute stone harp.

I 1: **Hugh Gaitskell** (1963), the Labour leader, has a very large urn on a substantial podium, all in Portland stone.

I 7: see H 6.

I 59: **Rosetta Bright** (1929), also has a large urn, much decorated with fruit on the base and a heap of sculpted flowers.

I 84A: **Temple Moore** (1920), the architect, has a composition headstone with a crucifixion scene, designed by his son-in-law, the architect Leslie T. Moore.

I 85: **Teresa Nécom** (1926) has an arch-shaped monument, like the top of a wishing well, and a crazy-paved garden in front.

I 104: **Frederick de Bertodano** (1955), of an ancient Spanish family, has a twelve-foot cross on an art-deco base which, at time of writing, is being swamped with ivy.

J 3: **Elsa Collins** (1962) has a scrolled headstone of Yugoslav Nabrazina; a heart-shaped plaque lies on the grave.

J 10: see C 29.

J 11: **Michael Llewelyn Davies** (1921), one of Barrie's Lost Boys, has a limestone headstone, part old, part new. The old bottom part is handsomely festooned.

J 14: see C 88.

J 30: **Emma Brooke** (1874) has an elegant Roman pedestal, decorated with rosettes, triglyphs, dentils and scrolls.

K 62: see A 54.

K 72: **Sarah Prance** (1847), as well as a coped bodystone, has a top-heavy marble headstone, dominated by praying cherubs.

K 78: see E 12.

L 93: **A.R. Orage** (1934), the writer and editor, has a slate ledger with a strange device, which he called 'a picture of man'. It has been described as 'a circle, divided by crisscross lines until it looked like a fly's eye'. The lettering is very distinguished.

M 69: see D 88.

Teresa Nécom

Randolph Schwabe

M 78: **Kate Walton** (1935) is one of several Odeon-style headstones hereabouts, some are decorated with lilies and other flowers.

M 80: see G 12.

M 83: see D 88.

N 109: **Randolph Schwabe** (1948), the artist, has a small statue of a female carrying a scroll; it is signed ALD 1951, and is by Alan Lydiat Durst (1883–1970), a fellow-member of the London Group.

P 93: **Gordon Byrne** (1961) has a headstone of composition material, which looks like limestone; it is topped by a sculpted plaque of rabbits and marguerites.

Q 91: **E.V. Knox** (1971), the editor of *Punch*, has a handsome headstone in green Northumberland slate with good lettering and a quotation from W.J. Cory's *Heraclitus*.

Q 83: **Sarah Pattinson** (1975) has the same material, embellished with fine lettering and scrolling.

3. Monuments in the Church

Most of these monuments are wall plaques and are of marble, unless otherwise stated. They are listed in order of reference numbers, which start at the south east end and go clockwise. Nos. CH 76 onwards are in the gallery.

Note that NADFAS produced a detailed report on the church monuments in 1984, which includes more technical descriptions and evaluations, e.g. of crests and materials.

CH 1: Anthony Askew, MD, FRS (1774), is one of the few eighteenth-century monuments: in fact, Lysons says that in 1796 (the date of his survey) it was the only monument in the church, and that it was at the 'west end where the communion table was'. This is curious, as most histories suggest that the altar was then at the east end and was not moved to the west end until 1878. The plain wall monument is topped with an urn and garland.

CH 2: Rev. Samuel White (1841), '34 years incumbent of this parish', has a voluminous marble surplice draped over his wall plaque. The sculptor is William Groves (born 1809), who exhibited at the Royal Academy from 1834 to 1861.

CH 5: Hon. David Erskine, Earl of Buchan etc., died in 1745, but his monument was not erected until about half a century later (c.f. Lysons, above). The erector was his famous grandson, Thomas, Lord Erskine, who lived locally. The fairly plain wall plaque has a fine crest, featuring a stork with a snake in its mouth.

CH 9: Dorothy Harrison (1802), wife of a barrister at Lincolns Inn, who became Assistant Secretary in the Treasury, has a monument sculpted and signed by R. Westmacott senior, Mount Street, London, This is presumably Richard Westmacott the Elder (1747–1808), father of the more famous Sir Richard (see CH 58). The Elder became Mason for Kensington Palace in 1796, but was bankrupt by 1803. The monument is small and simple, with a gravy-boat urn.

CH 13: Charles Duncan (1806) is one of four monuments signed by John Bacon the Younger (1777–1859). Son of an RA, Bacon began exhibiting at the Royal Academy from the age of 15. This monument of white marble on black has a conventionally draped urn, with cross and palm. The crest is topped by a three-masted ship.

CH 14: Sabina Tierney (1806) again displays the urn, that was so fashionable at this period, but hers is supported by two twisted snakes.

CH 16,17: Lownds (1811) and **Beresford** (1818) are also signed by J. Bacon Junr.: they are identical wall plaques, each with a broken lily on top.

CH 20: William Bleamire (1803) has a white and grey marble monument, signed by Joseph Kendrick (born 1755), showing a lady mourning over an urn.

CH 39: Rev. S.B. Burnaby (1902), 'vicar of this parish for 27 years', has a brass plaque, too high to read, signed by Jones & Willis.

CH 40: The **Selwyn** brothers, who include the first Bishop of New Zealand (died 1878), and Sir Charles Selwyn (1868), the eminent lawyer, have a monument in the Lady Chapel in the form of a piscina. This was set up by the Bishop's elder son in 1912 and incorporates the stem of the font used in this church when the brothers were baptised.

The Selwyn monument.

CH 43: **John Dixon** (1860) is one of several church benefactors commemorated in this corner of the church by plain brass plaques, signed by Hart Son Peard & Co. Ltd.

CH 44: **Alfred Bell** (1895), 'a liberal benefactor of this church', also has a brass tablet, signed by Jones & Willis.

CH 45: **John Keats**'s bust in the north transept was carved by Anne Whitney in 1883 and presented, in July 1894, by American admirers of the poet: the life-size bust, mounted on a carved console, was unveiled by Edmund Gosse. Sickert's painting of Aubrey Beardsley at the ceremony is in the Tate Gallery. According to Barratt, this bust is 'the first memorial to Keats raised on English soil'.

The Keats bust, an American gift.

CH 52: **John Rixton**, who died in 1658, has two marble slabs, which are the oldest monuments in the church and churchyard. Under the one on the floor of the north transept is 'interred ye corpse of John Rixton Gent'; this has a crest including three armillary spheres. The other stone, on the wall of the north-east porch, records his gifts to the poor (see Appendix). These are the only memorials preserved from the old (pre-1745) church.

CH 58: **'George Todd** Esq. of Bellsize' (*sic*), who died in 1829, has a monument with minimal decoration of acanthus and squirls, signed 'Richard Westmacott, London'. One of three eponymous sculptors, this is, according to Rupert Gunnis, Sir Richard Westmacott, the Royal Academician (1775–1856).

CH 59: **Haldimand** and CH 62 **Holford**, both dated 1817, have comparatively ornate wall plaques, at a time when so many were so merely classical. Holford's is signed by Humphrey Hopper (born 1767) who, according to Gunnis, produced 'a lamentable mass of marble' for General Hay's monument in St Paul's Cathedral in 1814.

CH 61: **Dobson Willoughby** (1833), whose name lingers on the Carlile Estate (see below), has a plain tablet, signed Patent Works, Westminster. They were mass producers of fireplaces and monuments, according to Gunnis, mostly dull and frequently ugly.

CH 64: **Edward Carlile** (1833), of the Carlile estate (off Rosslyn Hill) has a simple monument, signed by a local marble mason, John Field (1777–1843). Field, who lived and worked in Heath Street, is buried in the old churchyard (XH 032).

CH 67: **Mary Collings** (1817) has a wall plaque signed 'Ashton, Swallow St., London'. Of the two sculptors called Robert Ashton, father and son, this is probably the younger. The coat-of-arms includes, according to NADFAS, '3 torches or inflamed proper'.

CH 68: **Hester Stride** (1798), wife of a Manor Steward, has one of the oldest marble tablets in the church: it is topped by an urn with drapes.

CH 70: **Joanna Baillie** (1851) and her family have the plainest of monuments, signed 'T. Gaffin, Regent St'. Thomas Gaffin and his father, Edward, were, according to Gunnis, 'the most prolific statuaries of the first half of the nineteenth century, mostly tame and dull'.

CH 71: **Lucy Shout** (1822), being the wife of the sculptor, Robert Shout (1764–1843) of West Hampstead, has presumably him to thank for her extremely plain (unsigned) monument: or was it a prentice piece by her son, Charles (1795–1855), who is buried in the new graveyard (J 103)?

Rev. Thomas Ainger's memorial, designed by Sir George Gilbert Scott.

'not too unfortunate'. This must be one of those occasions, because the monument is liberally decorated and, apart from the usual draped urn, has a crest, scroll and lilies.

CH 76: **Henry Sharpe** (1873), a wealthy Portugal merchant, has a wall plaque in the gallery, 'raised by those who derived benefit in their youth from his disinterested efforts for their instruction and improvement'. This has a cameo profile of the great benefactor and is signed by G.G. Adams (1821–98), the distinguished statuary and medallist; he was the sculptor selected in 1852 to take the death-mask of the Duke of Wellington.

CH 77: **Hon. Frances Erskine** died in Hampstead in 1805, and four years later her husband, the great Lord Erskine, erected this handsome oval monument to her. It is signed by the prolific John Bacon the Younger (1777–1859) but, unlike his three other works in this church (CH 13, 16, 17), it

CH 73: **Rev. Thomas Ainger**, who died in 1863, has an exuberant design, very welcome among so many plain plaques, but perhaps surprising for a vicar of this church. The artist, according to Barratt, was Sir George Gilbert Scott, then resident at Admiral's House, and he has included a cameo profile of Ainger, surrounded by signs of the four evangelists. Decorations are in varied marbles and semi-precious stones.

CH 73A: **Henry Cort**, the great inventor, who died in Hampstead in 1800, is commemorated and pictured in a bronze bas relief plaque in the east porch. This was designed by A.E. Howard of Worcester and erected by an American admirer, Charles H. Morgan in 1906. Cort is buried in the graveyard (XB 018).

CH 75: **George Henry Errington** (1843), who claims lineage back to the time of the Conquest, has an elaborate memorial above the north east staircase to the gallery. This is signed by J. Bedford of 256 Oxford Street (died 1875), whose work, according to Gunnis, was mostly conventional but occasionally

Lord Erskine's wife.

is an elaborate affair. The inevitable urn has cherub-head handles, and is swagged with foliage, while the figures of Hope (with anchor) and Charity (with heart) flank the inscription.

CH 80: **Charles Cartwright** (1825), of the East India Company and Belsize Park, is another to have a monument by the local mason, John Field (see CH 64). The crest on this obelisk-shaped plaque is a wreath round a horse's head.

CH 87: **Thomas Norton Longman**, the publisher, died in 1842 after 42 years' residence in Hampstead. Three years later, a group of his friends erected this impressive memorial, which was designed by Christopher Moore (1790–1863). A decorated coffin is topped by a bust of Longman, resting on two books. (Picture on page 26)

CH 89: **William Baker** (1850) is commemorated by a tablet 'erected by members of the Hampstead Choral Society with whom he was intimately connected'. It is signed by Watts, Hampstead: this is presumably the William Watts, stonemason, of Perrins Lane, buried in A 106.

CH 91: **John Ranicar Park** (1847), a local surgeon, has a classical plaque, signed 'Denman, 83 Regent Street'. This is probably Thomas Denman, born 1787, brother-in-law of John Flaxman, whose designs he borrowed, according to Gunnis.

CH 95: **Rev. Edward Levett** (1845) has a crest with lion rampant and crossed swords. The tablet is signed R. Brown, 58 Great Russell St, London – presumably the Robert Brown, who flourished 1830–57, according to Gunnis.

Stained glass and paintings

Most of the windows in the church are also memorials, and most of the stained glass is by Clayton & Bell. Alfred Bell (q.v.) gave most of the windows to the church in 1878. One window in the gallery is dedicated to Sir George Gilbert Scott (CH 92), Bell's tutor, and another to Sir Thomas Maryon Wilson (CH 82), usually known as 'the villainous Lord of the Manor'.

The large painting of John the Baptist and other saints (CH 33) on the south wall (but soon to be moved to the Lady Chapel) is a copy of a Fra Filippo Lippi in the National Gallery; it serves as a memorial to the three grandsons of Alfred Bell who were killed in the first World War, 'for King, Country and Humanity'. The copy had been made in 1869 by Clement Burlison, Alfred's brother-in-law.

The reredos in the Lady Chapel (CH 39B) was painted in 1960 by the local artist, Donald Towner (1903–85), as a memorial to his mother, who is buried in the graveyard (XF 007). The oil picture shows Christ in mandorla, the Virgin and St John the Evangelist, with Church Row in the background.

The stained glass in the Lady Chapel (CH 41), dedicated to Frederick Haeffner, 'who fell in the battle of the Somme, 1916', is by Joan Fulleylove: the window is called The Crown of Life. The artist was the daughter of John Fulleylove, RI, and painted windows for, *inter alia*, the New Masonic Hall in London and Khartoum Cathedral.

V WHO WAS WHO

A biographical guide

In most cases, dates of birth have been calculated by subtracting the person's age from the date of death and may, therefore, be one year out.

All quotations are from monumental inscriptions, unless otherwise stated. DNB = Dictionary of National Biography.

ABEL James (1762–1817) bought a quarter of Belsize Park in 1807, including Belsize House; he lived in Frognal. (XE 131)

ABRAHAM, Robert (1773–1850), architect, of Keppel Street, Russell Square, 'executed works at Arundel Castle, the synagogue near the Haymarket, and the Westminster Bridewell' (DNB). (A 50/51)

ADAMS, James Blake (1749–1806), 'many years organist of this parish', lived in Windmill Hill. (XB 078)

ADAMS, John (1762–1831) 'was Beadle of this Parish for 28 years and, having most faithfully discharged the duties of his office, the Parish has caused this Stone to be placed to his Memory'. (XF 062)

ADAMS, Thomas Hewitt (1812–90), 'for 20 years verger and sexton at this church'; also a carpenter at 2 Church Place. (XH 013)

AGNEW, Major General William (1821–88), 'Bengal Staff Corps, Judicial Commissioner of Assam, and JP for the County of Middlesex'. Born in Larne; died at 6 Belsize Park Gardens. (D 24)

AIKIN, Lucy (1781–1864), authoress, niece and biographer of Mrs Barbauld, niece of Philip Le Breton (q.v.); lived in Church Row. (XB 124)

AINGER, Rev. Thomas (1799–1863), 'Prebendary of St Paul's, 22 years incumbent of this parish'; he was a vigorous vicar from 1841 until his death. In the early 1850s he organised the Dispensary for the Sick Poor in New End, where a tablet pays tribute to him still. (XB 223)

AITKEN, George (1860–1917), 'CB, MVO, the very mirror of a public servant, a scholar, a beloved and devoted husband', Assistant Secretary, Home Office, from 1892, Life Governor of University College, literary biographer and editor of e.g. Steele, Burns and Defoe. Died at 21 Church Row. (H 2)

AITKEN, George (died 1942: no relation to above?), 'Doctor of Music, Organist and Choirmaster'. He was recommended as organist by 'Father' Willis, who built the church organ in 1853, and he stayed far longer than any other organist here

– from 1895 until his death: he was also a composer and critic. He lived at 58 Gondar Gardens. (CH 38)

AKSAROVA-STURTZ, Valentina (1894–1959), Russian opera singer; she died at 12 Strathray Gardens. (P 92)

ANDERSON, Edward Philip (1883–1934), Lt/ Colonel, Royal Engineers: DSO, Chevalier Legion D'Honneur. Superintendent of Works, Khyber Railway, and in other Indian posts. From 1929 was Inspecting Officer of Railways, MOT. (N 70)

ARMITAGE, Rev. George (1810–1900), '39 years Vicar of Silverdale, Staffs', died at 5 Tanza Road, aged 90. His wife, **Martha**, died 28 years later, aged 93. Their epitaph begins curiously: 'They art thine, O Lord . . .' (B 95)

ASHBY, George Payne (1797–1872), grocer in the High Street, also Overseer of the Poor. (XB 146)

ASHLEY, Henry Victor (1872–1945), FRIBA, architect, won competition for new Freemasons Hall, Holborn, which he built 1931–3. Other works included French Bank in London, housing schemes, hospitals, etc. Designed 20 Frognal Gardens for himself c. 1926. Was churchwarden of Parish Church, rebuilt Moreland Hall and designed the Columbarium, which now contains his memorial plaque. (Col. E 3)

ASKEW, Anthony (1722–74), MD, FRS, classical scholar, physician to St Bartholomew's and Christ's Hospitals. Married daughter of Robert Halford, Master in Chancery, and had 12 children by her (DNB). Lived near Fenton House. (CH 1)

ATTWOOD, John (1720–1804), 'cornchandler of this parish', is buried with another cornchandler, of Hollybush Hill, who married his 'neice'. (XD 106)

AYRE, Rev. John (1801–69), born at Spalding, Lincs. 'During 20 years minister of St John's Chapel, Downshire Hill'. Lived in the High Street. (XD 183)

AYRES, Thomas (1798–1857) 'late of Jack Straws Castle' and the adjoining livery stables. (XB 050)

BAILLIE, Joanna (1762–1851) came with her family to Bolton House, Windmill Hill, in 1791. Her

Plays of the Passion in 1798 were a sensational success, and she was praised and visited by Byron, Scott and other literary lions. The most famous woman dramatist of her day, she died aged 88 at Bolton House, which now bears a plaque from the Royal Society of Arts. **Dorothea Baillie** (1720–1806), 'sister of the celebrated brothers William and John Hunter, relict of the Rev. James Baillie DD, Professor of Divinity in the University of Glasgow, mother of the eminent Physician Matthew Baillie, and of two daughters Agnes and Joanna, the latter being the distinguished authoress. All here were through life highly respected.' **Agnes Baillie**, who lived with her sister and mother at Bolton House, died there in 1861 aged 100. The family came from Lanarkshire. Matthew Baillie (1761–1823) was a 'morbid anatomist' (DNB) who became Physician to George III. William Hunter (1718–83) was Physician to Queen Charlotte: his museum was acquired by Glasgow University. John Hunter (1728–93) was Surgeon to George III: his collection was acquired by the Royal College of Surgeons. (XB 125, pictured on page 24, and CH 70)

BALL, Major Adrian Albert (1892–1965), DCM, of Melbourne, served with Australian troops in two world wars, including the Gallipoli campaign. He died at 3 Hampstead Mansions. (J 5)

BARNES, Henry (1703–73), 'one of the Secondaries of the Court of Common Pleas at Westminster and also an Attorney of the same Court the last 13 years of his Life. In this long Course of Business, he Ornamented and Honoured his Profession . . . etc.' He lived near Hampstead Square. (XD 138)

BARRS, Edith and Kate (died 1963, 1966), popular Sunday School teachers, lived at 20 Carlingford Road. (A 11)

BARTON, Mrs Rachel (1742–1813) was 'widow of Admiral Matthew Barton', who left his rank on Admiral's House and Walk, but in fact never lived there (see *Camden History Review 9*). His main local residence was Vane House, where he died in 1795; he was buried at St Andrew's, Holborn. (XJ 004)

BATTY, Herbert (1849–1923), in Indian Civil Service from 1868, Judge of High Court, Bombay, Professor of Logic and Moral Philosophy, Poona College, 1872–75. (H 76)

BEAUMONT, William Comyns (1879–1955), journalist, author and lecturer. Created and edited *The Bystander* magazine (later *The Graphic*), 1903. Was also Literary Editor of *Illustrated London News*, 1940. Lived at Providence Corner, Well Road. (O 90)

BEDINGFIELD, Daniel (d. 1637), 'Gentleman of Grays Inn'; 'Clerk of the Parliaments' says Lysons. (XL 028)

BELL, Alfred (1832–95), water colourist, stained glass designer and maker, 'for 16 years Churchwarden . . . a liberal benefactor to the church and a faithful friend to the clergy and congregation'. Nearly all the windows in the church were given by him and made by his firm, Clayton & Bell. He also designed a new font in 1885 and a new nave ceiling. Lived at Bayford House, Lyndhurst Terrace. (CH 44 and E 74) **John Clement Bell** (1860–1944), landscape and stained glass artist (? son of Alfred), died at 58 Fitzjohns Avenue. (E 70)

BELL, Edward (1844–1926), elder son of publisher George Bell (d. 1890) and chairman of the family firm, also President of the Publishers Association. Lived many years in Hampstead, finally at 6 The Mount. (F 10)

BENHAM, William Ash (1774–1813), grocer and cheesemonger in the High Street, and built the terrace called Benham's Place in 1813, the year he died; this may explain his early death. (XD 066)

BESANT, Sir Walter (1836–1901), novelist, antiquarian, social reformer, long resident in Hampstead at several addresses, notably Frognal End in Frognal Gardens (blue plaque). His grave is one of only four listed by the DOE. Besant's socially-conscious novels prompted the establishment of the People's Palace in Mile End. He was first chairman of the Society of Authors, started and edited *The Author*, and wrote a survey of London in ten vast volumes (DNB etc.). (C 64)

BIRKBECK, Charles John (1819–21), infant son of Dr George Birkbeck of Settle, Yorkshire, founder of mechanics' institutions, notably Birkbeck College (1824), also founder and councillor of University College, London (1827). (K 100)

BLACK-HAWKINS, Clive David (1915–83), joined University College School, Frognal, in 1938 and rose to be Headmaster, 1956–75. Died at 14A Wedderburn Road. His wife, **Ruth Eleanor** (1913–77), was a JP. (Col. E 4)

BLEAMIRE, William (1730–1803), 'many years one of His Majesty's Justices of the Peace and a member of the Honourable Society of Grays Inn' Barratt says 'the late philanthropic William Bleamire Esq. was founder of the Hampstead Parochial Benefit Society', which aimed at promoting 'Industry, Frugality and Sobriety among the labouring Class' (Park). The 1802 Directory shows him as 'Magistrate of Hatton Garden Police Office, Hampstead'. (CH 20 and 25)

BOOT, William Henry James (d. 1918), RI, landscape painter and illustrator, exhibited at RA 1874–84. He was Art Editor of *Strand Magazine* 1891–1910. He died at 1 Cannon Place. (I 28)

BOOTH, Nathaniel, Lord Delamer (1710–70), 'who after a long illness, which he bore with incredible Patience, died as he had lived with the utmost Calmness and Composure, the natural effect of a comfortable Review of his past life, and the near and joyful Prospect of a better'. Whig politician, appointed in 1727 as Surveyor of the Greenwax Money (a form of fine). In 1743 he married Margaret Jones of Covent Garden, and they lived at Burgh House until 1758, when he became the 4th (and last) Lord Delamer. He then lived at Dunham Massey (Cheshire), where the National Trust guidebook now says he was an 'unattractive man, who planted most of the finest trees'. (XD 092)

BOSANQUET, Charles (1769–1850), City merchant, Governor of South Sea Company, High Sheriff of Northumberland (1828). Colonel in Hampstead Volunteers. Lived at The Firs, near the Spaniards. (K 92–93)

BOYDELL, Nicolas (1781–8), son of Josiah Boydell, Esq., of West End. Josiah (1752–1817), City Alderman, painter and engraver, exhibited at RA 1772–99 (see DNB). Co-founder of Hampstead Volunteers. (XB 212)

BRAY, Mrs Anne (died 1776) offered her organ to the church in 1767, for 'accompanying the psalmody'. She played it there for the next 9 years and was voted £10 per annum for loan of it, and £30 per annum (later £40) for playing and tuning it and paying the blower. (XF 032)

BRIDGE, Isaac (1838–1905), 'for 11 years Vestryman of this Parish', corndealer and jobmaster, 22 King's College Road and Mews. (E 86)

BRIGGS, Professor Henry (1883–1935), OBE, FRSE, etc., Professor of Mining at Edinburgh University and at Heriot–Watt College. He was much involved in research for safety in mines and invented mine rescue apparatus. Published many books and learned papers. (M 81)

BRODRICK, William John Henry (1874–1964), OBE, barrister, Metropolitan Police Magistrate 1928–44, Chevalier, Order of the Crown of Belgium. Chairman of the Heath & Old Hampstead Society. Died at 12 Frognal Gardens. (0 87)

BROOKE, Leonard Leslie (1862–1940), artist and illustrator. Created the popular *Johnny Crow* books for children and illustrated many nursery rhyme books. He married **Sybil** 1890–1957, daughter of Stopford Brooke (q.v.). Their son,

Henry, was MP for Hampstead and Home Secretary, and they moved to 28 Hollycroft Avenue in 1934 to be near him. At the artist's own suggestion, he was buried by the local undertaker called J. Crowe. An exhibition, 'Leslie Brooke and Johnny Crow' was held at Burgh House in 1984. (0 77)

BROOKE, Stopford (1832–1916), Irish Minister of Proprietary Chapel, Bloomsbury, 1876–95. A celebrated preacher, in 1867 he became chaplain to Queen Victoria, but he seceded from the Anglican church in 1880. He often preached at Rosslyn Hill Chapel. Most successful among his books was his *Primer of English Literature*, 1876. (J 30)

BUCK, Thomas (1785–1847), victualler, leased the Holly Bush Tavern in 1831; he died at Twickenham, 'surviving his wife only a fortnight'. (D 106)

BUDD, James (1757–1820) 'was Nine Years Master of the Poorhouse of this Parish and, having most faithfully discharged the duties of his Office, the Parish has caused this Stone to be placed to his Memory' (c.f. John Adams). (XE 064)

BULL, Mrs Elizabeth (1674–1702), 'wife of Richard Bull of London, druggist, by whom she had issue, 3 sons and 8 daughters . . .' and died aged 28. (XG 019)

BURCK, Andrew (1790–1861), a Master Baker, who lived at No. 1 Church Row, and had a shop at 59 High Street. The latter may have suggested the old street name Baker's Row and the recent Baker's Alley. (XD 141)

BURGH, Rev. Allatson (1769–1856) lived at Burgh House from 1822 until his death. He was vicar of St Lawrence Jewry in the City and was so unpopular that his parishioners petitioned Queen Victoria to have him removed – in vain. Burgh was a more successful protestor himself in 1829, when he joined Hampstead copyholders fighting the Lord of the Manor over the Heath. (CR 12)

BURLISON, John (Senior) (1810–68) was son of a Durham joiner, who became personal assistant to Sir George Gilbert Scott for 25 years. His son (q.v.) was a stained glass maker. (E 77)

BURLISON, John (Junior) (1843–91) founded the famous stained glass firm of Burlison & Grylls (Mr Grylls lived at Burgh House). He is commemorated by a Clayton & Bell window in the church: Alfred Bell was his brother-in-law. (CH 54)

BURN, James (1727–94), DD, 'many years senior chaplain to the Presidency of Calcutta' . . . 'whose Character singularly united the Firm and manly with the gentler virtues'. (XB 158)

BURNABY, Rev. Sherrard Beaumont (died 1902), 'Vicar of this parish for 27 years, from 1873 to 1900'; he retired through ill health and died in Great Missenden. (CH 39)

BUSH, Thomas (died 1890?), headmaster of Heath Mount School in Heath Street until c. 1875. The school history says he was fond of wielding a bushy stick. (B 83)

BUTTERWORTH, Sir Alexander Kaye (1854–1946), grandson of Bishop Kaye of Lincoln (1827–53); General Manager of North Eastern Railway 1906–21, Director of Welwyn Garden City in 1930s. Lived at 16 Frognal Gardens and died aged 91. (F 105)

CAMPBELL, George (1785–1854), nurseryman and florist of Heath Street. Soon after his death, Campbell's Nursery Gardens were sold and the Baptist Chapel, Nos. 86–90 Heath Street, and Mansfield Place were built on the site. (XF 002)

CARLILE, Edward (1766–1833), rich haberdasher of Bow Lane, who in 1814 bought a large estate in the Willoughby Road area. His daughter Janet married into the Willoughby family, who developed the Carlile estate in the 1870s. (K 75)

CARNEY, George Arthur Thomas (1887–1947), actor and music-hall comedian, whose films included *The Stars Looked Down*. He is buried with his wife, **Dorothy** (died 1948) and the motto on their gravestone is the mysterious 'Buckling and Skung'. They lived at 67 Fitzjohns Avenue. (M 106)

CARR, Thomas William (1770–1829), 'of Frognal in this Parish and Eshott in Northumberland, FRS, FGS etc., Barrister at Law, Treasurer of the Hon. Society of Grays Inn, for 25 years His Majesty's Solicitor of Excise. In the management of important changes effected in the excise revenue he was uniformly distinguished by his talent and zeal for the public good' etc. etc. He lived at Maryon Hall, Frognal Lane. (K 84)

CARSWELL, Donald (1882–1940), 'born Glasgow ... killed in a blackout accident in London 1940, he was journalist, barrister, biographer, critic, playwright, Civil Servant, devoted lover and true friend', husband of **Catherine Carswell** (1878–1946) 'of Glasgow ... poet, critic and biographer, wife, mother and courageous friend ... full of eager spirit'. The Carswells were close friends and helpers of D. H. Lawrence, about whom Catherine wrote a memoir, *Savage Pilgrimage* (1932). They lived many years at Holly Bush House, Holly Mount. (H 12)

CARTER, John (1748–1817), 'Antiquarian, Draftsman, Architect and Fellow of the Society of Antiquaries of London. He was distinguished for his ... superior knowledge of the Ancient Architecture of England ... His zeal for the preservation of Ancient Buildings and remains of Antiquity was equal to his judgment and science, and he had the high satisfaction of knowing that his active and steady Perseverance had been the means of saving from Destruction several ancient structures, valuable monuments of the skill of our ancestors.' He is credited with saving the Galilee and the Neville Screen at Durham Cathedral in 1796, according to Colvin, who says he was nervous, irascible and eccentric. Among his many publications, mostly views of Gothic buildings, he had printed pseudonymously a dramatic account of an unhappy love affair, illustrated by an engraving of his inamorata in the nude (DNB). (XE 055)

CARTWRIGHT, Charles (1753–1825), 'Accountant General to the Honourable East India Company, whom he served with distinguished ability and integrity for the period of 54 years': he lived at Upper Bartrams in Haverstock Hill. (CH 80)

CARY, Robert (1681–1751) was a Virginia merchant, who owned much property in Hampstead. (See also 'Puzzles and Blunders' above.) (XE 061)

CASTLEDEN, Rev. James (1778–1854) came to Hampstead in 1817 and started Baptist services in the Holly Mount chapel the following year; 'he was for 40 years a faithful minister of the gospel in this town'. (XI 009)

CHAMPNEYS, Basil (1842–1935), architect and author, son of a Dean of Lincoln. His buildings included Newnham College, Cambridge, and the Rylands Memorial Library, Manchester. Locally he was responsible for St Luke's, Kidderpore Avenue, and another St Luke's in Kentish Town. In 1881, he built Hall Oak, Frognal Lane, for himself and died here aged 92. He married a daughter of the Hon. Adelaide Drummond (q.v.). (M 80)

CHARLES, Elizabeth Rundle (1827–96), authoress of a popular children's book, *Chronicles of the Schoenberg-Cotta Family* (1862). Her house in Oak Hill Way bears her plaque. (A 35)

CLARKE, Henry (1832–1914), chairman of local magistrates, lived at Cannon Hall. (B 71)

CLEWS, William (died 1849), tailor and Heath protector (1829). (XI 021)

CLOWSER, George (1852–1916), eldest son of Thomas Clowser, whose building firm was busy in

Victorian Hampstead – e.g. building Oak Hill Park in the 1850s. Their office was at 27 High Street (lately Knowles Brown). (H 24)

COATES, Christopher Joseph (1820–1905) ran China & Glass Warehouse at 33 High Street, also Registrar of Marriages, Rate Collector and Secretary of the New End Dispensary for 22 years. He built 26 Willoughby Road, which bears his monogram, in 1883, and lived there unto death. His wife, **Elizabeth**, took in lodgers, when they lived over their High Street shop: these included in 1852 Ford Madox Brown. (XJ 002)

COLE, Benjamin (1782–1843) bought an estate and messuage in Frognal near the church in 1820, including a pond, known locally as Cole's Pond. It was mainly used for watering horses. (D 102)

COLERIDGE, Berkeley and Florence (d. 1834), grandchildren of the poet. His daughter Sara married her cousing Henry Coleridge in 1829, and they lived in Downshire Hill until 1837. These infants died in January 1834, six months before their grandfather, who with his family was then buried in Highgate. (F 90–108)

COLLINS, John, Senior (1759–1827), dairy farmer at North End. His family ran Collins Farm (Wyldes) from 1793 to 1854 (E 46). **John** junior (1782–1858), son of the above, 'of The Farm, North End', has his name scratched on a window at Wyldes. He let rooms from at least 1823, when his lodger was the artist John Linnell – see plaque on house. (XB 114)

COLLINS, Sir William Job (1859–1946), 'KCVO, MD, MS, FRCS, sometime Chairman of the LCC, Vice Chancellor of London University and a Member of Parliament'. He was Liberal MP for St Pancras (West) 1906–10, and for Derby 1917–18. He was also consulting surgeon to two eye hospitals, President of many societies (e.g. Huguenot Society), Chairman of many committees (e.g. Hop Industry) and wrote many books (e.g. *The Aetiology of the European Conflagration*). (J 20)

COLVIN, Sir Sidney (1845–1927), literary and art critic, author of several books on Keats, Keeper of Prints and Drawings at British Museum. In 1903 married **Frances**, widow of Rev. Albert Hurt Sitwell: 'she shared Colvin's intimacy with R.L. Stevenson' (DNB). Colvin brought the sickly Stevenson to Abernethy House, Mount Vernon, on several occasions for a Hampstead health cure. (I 30)

Sir Sidney Colvin

CONNON, John (died 1874), 'Chief Magistrate of Bombay, who died at Alexandria on his return voyage on 28 May 1874 and was buried in the Protestant Cemetery at Alexandria. (XE 052)

CONSTABLE, John (1776–1837), RA, much-loved landscape painter from Suffolk, many of whose views of Hampstead can be seen at the Tate and V & A. He took summer lodgings in Hampstead for his family from 1819 at various addresses, including 2 Lower Terrace and 25 Downshire Hill. From 1827 he installed his family at 40 Well Walk (now plaqued), and stayed there until his death. His wife Maria died tragically young in 1828 and was the first to be buried in the graveyard, 'leaving 7 infant children to lament her loss, in common with their surviving parent'. The artist and all his children are buried with her, except the eldest son, John. (See Appendix for full inscription) (XC 002)

COOK, John (died 1813), 'victualler; Coach & Horses. (XI 021)

COOPER, Henry (1877–1947), DSO, Surgeon in Royal Navy from 1904, Hon. Surgeon to George V 1930–32, Registrar to Soc. of Apothecaries of London 1932–39; Group Captain, RAF Medical Service in World War II; lived at 6 Holly Place. (Col. E 5)

John Constable by Reinagle, c. 1799.

CORT, Henry (1740–1800) of Devonshire Street, 'to whom the world is indebted for the arts of refining iron by puddling with mineral coal, and of rolling metals in grooved rolls'. So says the plaque in the church porch (see previous section). His tombstone says: 'He passed away a broken hearted man.' In 1789, six years after he had patented his revolutionary processes for purifying iron, Cort was ruined by his partner's embezzlement. Eight years later, his daughter died and, says Barratt, 'he retired to Hampstead a broken man'. His tomb has been renovated by the Institution of Civil Engineers and, in 1983 (the bicentenary of his invention), a chaplet was laid on it by the Historical Metallurgy Society. (CH 73A and XB 018)

COTTS, Sir William Dingwall Mitchell (1872–1932), 1st Baronet 1921, MP for Western Isles 1922/3, Head of Mitchell, Cotts & Co., merchants, colliery proprietors and steamship owners. Lived at 31 Redington Road. His son, **Sir William Campbell Mitchell-Cotts** (1902–64), who assumed the hyphen in 1932, was a director of Frederick Muller Ltd. (V 5)

CROCKER, Walter Henry (1885–1953), tobacconist of 4A Perrins Court, who became W.H. Crocker & Son, newsagents, at 7 Heath Street from the 1920s to the 1970s. (I 23)

CUNNINGTON, Thomas (1798–1866), butcher, of 55 High Street, and 'meat salesman to Her Majesty' in 1840 Directory. (XD 168)

CURWEN, John Spencer (1847–1916), FRAM, eldest son of John Curwen, inventor of the Tonic Sol-Fa System. Editor of *Musical Herald* from 1866. Lived at 49 Frognal. (I 9)

DALRYMPLE-HAY, Sir Harley (1861–1940), civil engineer, designed and constructed the Bakerloo, Piccadilly and Hampstead tube lines. Died at 57 Frognal. (XF 009)

DALTON, Sir Cornelius Neale (1842–1920), KCMG, CB, was in the Civil Service from 1873. From 1897–1909, he was Comptroller General of Patents, Designs and Trademarks. He died at 57 Belsize Avenue. (I 87)

DAVENPORT, Burrage (1777–1863) and **Hannah** (1782–1857) lived at 25 Church Row, 1819–39. Keats mentions a visit to their house in a letter to his brother George, 1819. (XH 009)

DAVIES, Arthur Llewelyn (1863–1907), barrister, married **Sylvia** (1866–1910), second daughter of George du Maurier (q.v.). Their 5 sons met J.M. Barrie in Hyde Park in 1897, and inspired his *Peter Pan* (1903). When their parents died tragically young, Barrie adopted them. Their story has been told in a biography and dramatised for television as *J.M. Barrie and the Lost Boys*. Two of the boys also died young – one in Flanders and the other bathing at Oxford. (J 2). They are all buried near the du Maurier grave. (Picture on page 10)

DAVIES, Rev. John Llewelyn (1826–1916), father of Arthur (above) and sometime vicar in St Marylebone and in Kirkby Lonsdale. In his 90 years, he was also chaplain to King George V, an early member of the Alpine Club, and a champion of unpopular causes, such as higher education for women. In the latter he was supported by his famous feminist daughter, Margaret, who nursed him in his final years at 11 Hampstead Square. (K 1)

DAVY, Catherine (died 1783), wife of 'Wm Davy Esq.', Premier Sergeant at Law to His Majesty'. He defended the runaway slave Sommersett against the claims of the slave owner in 1772. The Davys lived at Burgh House between 1768 and 1776. (XD 171)

DE BAUFRE, Joseph, junior (1754–1823), a Guardian of the Poor, raised £1,200 with Samuel Hoare and another to buy a new and better Poorhouse about 1800. From this workhouse developed the present New End Hospital. (XE 160)

DE BERTODANO, Frederick Ramon (1871–1955), 8th Marquis del Moral, born in New South Wales and served with the Notts Yeomanry. Bertodanos were one of the ancient families of Spain; the gold chain on their crest commemorated the ancestors who fought the Moors in 1212 and broke their chain defences. The family became anglicised after the 5th Marquis married an Englishwoman and became Governor of the Bank of England 1835–36. (I 104)

DE CONTI, Lady Janetta (1759–80), 'daughter of Rt. Hon. Cosimo Conte de Conti, a noble Toscan (*sic*) by birth, and Count of Holy Roman Empire'. Her grandfather was 'of the family of Lord Rollo and His Majesty's Agent and Consul General at the City and Kingdom of Tripoli'; his wife was 'of the families of the Earls of Ross and Seaforth'. (CR 1)

DEEDES, Rev. Brooke (died 1922), 'Vicar of this Parish 1900–13, Archdeacon of Hampstead 1912–20'. He had also been Archdeacon of Lucknow, 1892–7. (CH 39A)

DIXON, John (1790–1860), 'Churchwarden of this church 1831–36'; he was a bootmaker at 30 High Street. (CH 43 and XB 047)

DOWSE, William (1777–1859) ran livery and landau stables from 32 Flask Walk. His daughter, **Mary Farey** (1815–60) married the publican of the Ram Inn, Smithfield. (D 7)

DREAPER, William Porter (1868–1938), OBE, Founder and Hon. Sec. of the League of Science, Bibliographer for the Science Museum, Patentee of improvements in artificial silk, electrotyping etc., Editor of *Chemical World*. Died at 27 Willow Road. (O 68)

DRUMMOND, Hon. Adelaide (1828–1911), writer and illustrator, eldest daughter of 2nd Baron Ribblesdale, step-daughter of Lord John Russell (Prime Minister), wife of Maurice Drummond CB (1825–91), Disraeli's Private Secretary, Police Receiver and author. The Drummonds lived at several addresses in Hampstead, notably Rosslyn Hill, where their son **Lister** (1856–1916) was born. He was a barrister. Police Magistrate and Knight of the Order of St Gregory. (C 11)

DU MAURIER, George Busson (1834–96), *Punch* cartoonist and author of *Trilby* and other novels; he lived most of the last half of his life in Hampstead, which reminded him of his birthplace, Paris. From 1870–74 he was at 27 Church Row, and from 1874–95 at New Grove House, Hampstead Grove, which bears his plaque. The motto on his grave comes from the end of *Trilby*: 'A little trust that, when we die, we reap our sowing – and so,

George du Maurier

Sir Gerald du Maurier

goodbye!' The grave includes a memorial for George's elder son, Lieut-Colonel **Guy Louis Busson du Maurier** (1865–1915), DSO, Royal Fusiliers, killed in action in Flanders; he wrote a sensational patriotic play in 1909, *An Englishman's Home*, which his famous brother, Sir Gerald (q.v.) produced. **Sir Gerald Hubert Edward Busson du Maurier** (1873–1934), younger son of George; actor-manager (one of the last), created many roles, including Captain Hook in *Peter Pan*; managed Wyndham's Theatre 1910–25. He was born in Church Row and inherited his father's love of Hampstead. From 1916 until his death, he lived at Cannon Hall, where his daughter, the novelist Daphne, grew up. (I Bay)

DUNCAN, Charles (1739–1807), 'of Strathblaine in Scotland. At the age of 20 he settled as a merchant in Virginia. . . . Having in 1801 lost the loved partner of his life and, soon after, his eldest daughter, in company with the youngest, then languishing under a fatal illness, he revisited his native land . . . whither he was led by an affectionate wish once more to see his only surviving daughter . . .' (CH 13)

EARL, George Samuel Windsor (1813–65), 'Assistant Resident Councillor and Police Magistrate . . . died at Penang'. Scholar and Far Eastern explorer, Earl was born at North End, Hampstead, and went to sea at an early age. He was concerned with the colonisation of Indonesia, a name he invented. His father, **Percy** (1770–1827), was captain of the East India ship *Aurora*. His brother, also **Percy** (1809–46), was drowned in the Torres Strait. His mother, **Elizabeth** (1779–1874), died at Wildwood, North End, aged 95. (D 54)

EICKHOFF, Frederick Alexander (died 1959) was a butcher in Flask Walk, who dropped his German surname in World War I to avoid persecution, and traded under the name Frederick Alexander. (C 36)

END, James (1785–1840), publican and livery stableman at Freemasons Arms. (C 38–47)

ERRINGTON, George Henry (1783–1848), 'formerly of Cotton Hall (Staffs) and late of Colchester . . . of direct lineage from the ancient family of the Erringtons of Errington in the County of Northumberland, who were seated there at the time of the Conquest.' (CH 75 and A 46)

ERSKINE, Rt Hon. David, Earl of Buchan, Lord Cardross, Lord Auchterhouse, etc., etc., (1672–1745): 'This stone was erected to his memory by his grandson, Thomas, Lord Erskine, an inhabitant of this parish' (see below). (CH 5)

ERSKINE, Hon. Frances (died 1805), wife of Thomas, Lord Erskine (1750–1823), brilliant Scots barrister and Lord Chancellor. He was 20 when he married her, and they had 4 sons and 4 daughters. From 1788 they lived at Evergreen Hill, later called Erskine House, near the Spaniards Tavern. Her elaborate monument in the church is by John Bacon junior. (CH 77)

ESCOTT, Frederick William (1865–1928), local furniture dealer, first at 10 Flask Walk, later at 23 High Street. His twin daughters, who are buried with him, both died in 1918 aged 22. (I 26)

EVANS, Herbert Norman (1802–77); local doctor, lived at New Grove House for many years. Among his patients and friends was Constable, who painted his portrait in 1829. (XE 051)

FARJEON, Eleanor (1881–1965), author and poet, writer of children's books and, with her brother Herbert, of musical plays and revues. Her poetry included *Morning has broken*, now a popular hymn. She was born at 13 Adelaide Road and died at 20 Perrins Walk. (H 104)

FENN, Joseph (1793–1862) and eponymous son and grandson were tailors at 23 High Street over about a century, as shown by directories from 1823 to 1910. (XD 152)

FENTON, Philip (1735–1806), 'eminent merchant of Riga in the Empire of Russia', came to Fenton House in 1793 and, 'after a well spent life, he died at his House at Hampstead'. His nephew, **James** (1755–1834) inherited the property. Both took an interest in local affairs: it was James who convened the first Heath protection meeting in 1829. (XF 011)

FIELD, John (1776–1843), marble mason and builder of Heath Street. He has signed two tablets in the church, CH 64 and CH 80. (XH 032)

FIGGIS, Samuel (1841–1920), born in Dublin, came to Hampstead in 1885 and lived at Pitt House, North End. From c. 1910 lived at Montagu Grove, Frognal. He was a local conservationist and prime mover in saving Golders Hill Park for the public. (I 100)

FINCH, Edward (1695–1773) tenant of West End Farm, in 1762 Survey. (XE 039)

FITZGIBBON, Captain R.Q. (1809–71), 'late of Castle Grace House, Bangalore, India, who, after 44 years' service in the East, landed in England July 1st and fell asleep in Jesus July 31st, 1871.' (XB 69)

FLETCHER, Sir John Samuel (1841–1924), 1st baronet, barrister, JP, LCC Councillor 1889–1904, MP for Hampstead 1905–18, Chairman, Hampstead Board of Guardians 1880–98. Lived in College Crescent. (F 55)

FOLKARD, Abraham, Senior (1715–88), was one of Hampstead's philanthropic Philo-Investigists (see p. 48) and also a keen defender of the Heath, who led the attack on Mrs Lessingham's attempts to build Heath Lodge (see Park). Mrs Lessingham (q.v.) is buried in the same patch of the graveyard. (XD 043)

FORSTER, Matthew (1786–1869), merchant, shipowner and underwriter; MP for Berwick on Tweed 1841–53: he was also a reformer and an advocate of Free Trade. He contributed to the abolition of the West African Slave Trade by importing palm oil from the area for lubricating railway axles. This proved more profitable to the African chiefs than exporting their own people as slaves. Forster lived at Belsize House from the 1830s. (XB 215)

FORSTER, Thomas (1761–1816), 'victualler of this parish'; he was landlord of the White Horse on South End Green. (XB 110)

Matthew Forster and (immediately behind on the right) Jane Austen's aunt (see Hancock).

GAITSKELL, Rt Hon. Hugh Todd Naylor (1906–63), Leader of the Labour Party 1955–63. Lived many years at 18 Frognal Gardens which, in 1950 when Chancellor of the Exchequer, he preferred to 11 Downing Street. Motto on grave: 'Fortitudo et Integritas'. (I 1)

GAMBLE, Richard (1788–1863), baker in Heath Street, 'many years churchwarden of this parish'. (XB 021)

GANDER, William (no date) was R.L. Stevenson's landlord at Abernethy House, Mount Vernon, when he lodged there in the 1870s. (A 7)

GARDNOR, Thomas (1685–1775) built Gardnor House, 1736, and with his rich wife owned much property in the New End and Flask Walk area, including the Flask Tavern and the Bear Inn. He was also a Trustee for the Mineral Waters. (XB 011)

GIBSON, Thomas (1759–1832), banker of Newcastle-on-Tyne. His daughter, Jane, married secondly Sir Percy Florence Shelley, son of the poet and Mary Godwin: she was the friend of many eminent literary Victorians and edited the Shelley papers (1859). (J 100A)

GIDDEN, Lt/Cmdr Ernest Oliver (1910–61), GC, OBE, GM, RNVR, 'our darling Mick', won his George Cross for defusing a parachute mine on Hungerford Bridge in 1942. His obituary in *The Times* noted that when he arrived on the scene, trains and sleepers at Charing Cross were alight, as was the hotel. Tubes had been stopped and many local buildings, including the War Office, had been evacuated. After 6 hours' work, during which the timing mechanism began to tick, Gidden prised out the fuse with a chisel: for this he was awarded the George Cross, having previously won the George Medal. He was educated at UCS and lived at 21 Elsworthy Road. (L 62)

GIFFARD, Maj. Gen. Gerald Godfrey (1868–1926), 'of Guernsey, KCIE, CSI, KHS, IMS'. He was surgeon, mostly in Madras, also Professor of Midwifery and other Government appointments in India. (G 62)

GODFREY, William (1698–1766), 'one of His Majesty's Justices of the Peace for this County . . . with a strong natural genius and a very retentive memory'. (XB 167)

GOLDSMITH, Bishop Frederick (1853–1932), 'first Bishop of Bunbury, Western Australia', Vicar of Hampstead 1917–26. In Australia, he pressed for nationalisation of the Anglican Church and was awarded the VD (Volunteer Decoration). He was Rural Dean of Hampstead, 1917–21. (G 55)

GORE-BOOTH, Eva (1870–1926), Irish poet,

best remembered for *The Little Waves of Breffny*, and suffragette. W.B. Yeats dedicated a poem to her and to her sister, the Irish activist, Countess Markiewicz. Lived at 14 Frognal Gardens. (B 27)

GOSSETT, Jacob (1702–88) lived in Church Row and was elder brother of the famous Isaac Gosset (*sic* in DNB), who modelled portraits in wax. (XD 079)

GOULDING, William (1813–78), landlord of the Duke of Hamilton (in 1854 and 1873 Directories); probably related to Gouldings of Golden Yard. (XB 058)

GRANT, Sir Alexander (1746–1825), 7th Baronet, of Dalvey in Scotland, and his son, Sir Alexander Cray Grant, 8th Baronet (1781–1854), who was a West Indian planter and, as MP, represented planters' interests in the Commons. (CH 12)

GRANT, Rev. Charles (1746–1811), joint curate of Hampstead from 1793, and proprietor of the Chapel in Well Walk for about 30 years, says Park, who notes he was 'punctual and cheerful . . . His knowledge of the inferior orders of the parishioners was peculiarly extensive and accurate, and rendered him highly useful in a parish overflowing with poor'. He lived in Frognal. (XD 061)

GRAY, Joseph (1833–1906), civil servant, lived at Burgh House from 1902. His granddaughter, Angela Latham (1894–1980), an artist, died in Oak Hill Park. She and her husband, Peter Latham (1894–1970), who was Gresham Professor at London University, had previously lived at Frognal Rise. (C 35)

GREEN, Jonathan (1800–73), 'late of the Old White Horse' (Fleet Road). His second wife came from the Europa Tavern, Battersea. (XI 010)

GREEN, Mrs. Mary (1748–89) was a Miss Wadham, descendant of the founders of Wadham College, Oxford. Her husband, Valentine Green, was an eminent mezzotint engraver and Keeper of the British Institution in Pall Mall. (XB 209)

GREEN, Mary (1827–54), wife of architect T.K. Green (1831–1916), whose Gothic designs still liven up the Arkwright Road area; he built the eccentric 2 Ellerdale Road for himself about 1890. (D 11)

GREGORY, Professor F. Gugenheim (1893–1961), FRS, Professor of Plant Physiology at Imperial College of Science and Technology. Died at 8A Worsley Road. (Col. E 3)

GRIFFITH, Edward (1790–1858), 'FRS, of 32 Fitzroy Square, for many years one of the Masters of H.M. Court of Common Pleas at Westminster'. DNB adds that he was a naturalist and an original member of the Zoological Society. (E 92)

GRIFFITH, Richard Clewin (1872–1965), British Chess Champion, 1912; Hampstead Borough Councillor 1928–37; lived in Wedderburn Road 1890–1939. (Col. E 3)

GROVE, Stephen (1711–94), landlord of the Coach & Horses in Heath Street. (XB 103)

GUYON, Stephen (1707–79), son of a Huguenot refugee, came to Hampstead c. 1750 and lived in 5–6 The Mount, possibly at 98 Heath Street, still called Guyon House, and finally at Frognal Hall. He was great-grandfather to the General Richard Guyon, who fought in the 1848 Hungarian Uprising and had a street named after him in Budapest. (XE 009)

HAINES, William George (died 1958), songwriter and publisher, lyric writer of some of Gracie Fields hits. Lived 40 years at 13 Elsworthy Road. (L 103)

HAMMERSLEY, Mary (Mollie), née Grant (1863–1911), eldest of 3 sisters immortalised in pictures by Sargent, Augustus John and others. Her tuberculosis caused the Hammersley family to seek the healthy air of Hampstead. They lived at Admiral's House from 1902 and were noted for their literary/artistic salon. (A 66)

HANCOCK, Philadelphia (1730–92) was Jane Austen's aunt. With her is buried the author's cousin/sister-in-law, Elizabeth Austen, who died in 1813. It seems probable that Mrs Hancock came to Hampstead to consult doctors about her breast cancer; also that Jane Austen came to Hampstead to visit this grave, soon after Elizabeth's death. The original, much worn inscription (see Appendix) has recently been recut by the Jane Austen Society in a shorter form. (XB 211)

HANKINS, Thomas (1786–1832) was an Overseer of the Poor, who in 1825 oversaw some of them making the Leg o'Mutton Pond, later nicknamed Hankins's Folly. His wife was a tobacco and waxchandler in Heath Street. (XE 156)

HARE, Sir John (1844–1921), actor-manager, 'helped to mould and develop the modern English acting tradition' (DNB). He was manager of the Court Theatre from 1875, the St James from 1879, and he opened and managed the Garrick Theatre 1889–94. (J 10)

HARRISON, John (1693–1776) was the inventor of the marine chronometer or, as his inscription says, 'INVENTOR of the TIME-KEEPER for ascertaining the LONGITUDE at sea'. Buried with him is his son, William, FRS (1728–1815), who tested his chronometers on sea voyages and helped his father in the long struggle to claim his £20,000

John Harrison, 'the man who discovered longitude'.

prize. Their story is told graphically in the grave's own words, which are quoted in full in the Appendix. (XE 007)

HARRISON, Kay Kendall (1927–59), 'deeply loved wife of Rex'; actress, notably in the 1953 film, *Genevieve*. Her stone has fine lettering and decoration by Reynolds Stone. (H 4)

HART, Thomas, landlord of the Flask Tavern. His four children all died within a decade (1860–70). Their names and ages were Marian Maria 7, Annie Louisa 5, Mary Genie 3, and Young Thomas Spill (*sic*) 11 months. (XD 090)

HATELY, James, senior (1783–1857) was ironmonger, blacksmith and whitesmith in Heath Street. His grandson, **James Hately, junior** (1816–98), was a farrier and locksmith in Yorkshire Grey Yard. (XD 002)

HAWARD, Henry (1802–88), 'many years of the Flask Tavern in this parish'; he was publican for at least 29 years and owned property in Holly Mount. (XB 001)

HAYES, Thomas (1751–87), surgeon, 'blessed with native talents, emulous, diligent . . .' Park adds that he 'raised himself, solely by his own merit, from the low situation of a pot boy'. The three triangles on his tombstone show that he was a member of the local benevolent club, the Philo-Investigists (see p. 48). (XE 15A)

Henry Haward of the Flask Tavern.

HEMMING, George Wirgman (1821–1905), QC, law reporter and mathematician, who published work on calculus (DNB). Lived at 3 Fairfax Road. (F 77)

HEPBURN, Edith Alice Mary (1884–1947) wrote poetry under name Anna Wickham, was friend of D.H. Lawrence and his circle. Lived at 49 Downshire Hill from 1909 and at 68 Parliament Hill from 1919. (G 56)

HERKLOTS, Rev. Gerard Andreas (1833–1915), 'for 40 years vicar of St Saviour's, Hampstead', 1872–1912; he was previously assistant curate at the parish church. (G 94)

HILL, Ellen Gertrude (1841–1928) and her sister **Constance** (1844–1929), nieces of Sir Rowland Hill, lived for many years at 110 Frognal and previously with their father at 27 Thurlow Road. Constance was a writer, Ellen a portrait painter, who also ran a servants' home at No. 1 New End Square. (E 89)

HINDLEY, John (1753–1807), 'who under peculiar Disadvantages, which to common minds would have been a bar to any exertions, raised himself from all obscure situations of birth and

70

fortune by his own industry and frugality to the enjoyment of a moderate competency'. His full inscription is quoted in the Appendix. Baines called it the quaintest of all the church's memorials and noted that it was repaired (c. 1880) by the vicar and Manley Hopkins (father of the poet). According to this, only his ashes are buried here, a curiously early example of cremation. (XG 001)

HODGSON, John (1779–1858), 'of The Elms, Hampstead Heath, and St Helen's Place, London'. The Elms was on the site of St Columba's Hospital. The Hodgsons came of an old Hampstead family and lived to great ages – John to his 80th year, and his wife **Caroline** (born 1788) to her 98th year. (XC 006)

John Hindley

HOLFORD, Charles (1774–1838), leading member of benevolent local family, who lived at Holford House near Holford Road (see *Camden History Review No. 6*). He was active with the Hampstead Volunteers, the Public Library, Heath protests, and a Guardian of the Poor: he left £100 to the poor of the parish. His friendship with Constable

prompted the artist to give his famous lectures on landscape painting at the Assembly Rooms in Holly Bush Hill. (K 86)

HOLFORD, Josiah (1727–1817), a City merchant, 'lived many years in this Parish, highly respected and esteemed'. He was father of Charles (above), President of the Philo-Investigists (see p. 48) and responsible for many local benefactions, especially the Parish School. He died aged 90 at Holly Hill House (site of UCS Junior School). (CH 62)

HONEY, Laura (1816–43): an actress and singer, of whom the DNB says: 'Her performances were confined to the lightest class of entertainment.' (XC 008)

HOOKE, William (1751–1819), painter, of Windmill Hill. 'He was a lineal descendant of the celebrated Dr Robert Hooke. Though he soared not to any literary excellence like his ancestor, yet he passed with esteem through the vale of this humble life and died respected by his friends and neighbours.' Robert Hooke (1635–1703) was an eminent scientist, surveyor of London, designer of Montague House, etc., and inventor of a marine barometer (DNB). (XF 052)

HOPKINS, Felix, died Christmas Day, 1853, aged

Felix, brother of Gerard Manley Hopkins.

22 months: brother of Gerard Manley Hopkins. Their family lived in Oak Hill Park from 1852 to 1886: the father was a churchwarden. Did Gerard get inspiration for his poem, *Felix Randall*, from his brother's name and from the name on the next grave, Randall? (XE 105)

HOWARD, Gerrard (1709–81), JP, Deputy Lieutenant of Middlesex, resident in Church Row, married (secondly) a relation of Paravicini Mawhood, mentioned in Boswell's *Johnson*. Their daughter, Rebecca Elizabeth (1764–1801), married a prosperous clothier and army contractor, (Sir) James Duberly, from whom she eloped with Major General John Gunning, brother of the famous beautiful sisters (see DNB, Walpole Letters, etc.) (XB 198)

HUME, Eliza Ann (1807–56), daughter of Taverner Wallis (q.v.), left income from £90 Consols to be applied every third year to maintain her tomb; any surplus to be given to the poor of the parish. (The tomb was crumbling in 1984 and much repaired.) (XE 158)

HUMPHRIES, Rev. Francis (died 1792), curate of Hampstead for 30 years. (XL 028)

HUNT, Clara Leigh (1822–47), second wife (?) of Percy Bysshe Shelley Leigh Hunt, one of the many children of the poet, who lived in the Vale of Health c. 1815–21. Percy was at 3 Holly Hill in the 1850s. (I 35)

HUNT, Frederick (1805–52), '28 years sexton of this parish' (unless the inscription is wrong, he became sexton at 19). He is in the 'family grave of Thomas Hunt', who was the local Constable and a witness at a Chalk Farm duelling trial in 1818. (XF 063)

HUNTER, Rev. John (1848–1917), Scots Congregational Minister, Trinity Church, Glasgow: published many sermons and hymns. Died at 8 Prince Arthur Road. (G 1–3)

HURRELL, John (1756–1827), a High Street shopkeeper, who also worked the sandpits on the Heath. After his death, his wife and daughter (Jane) took over. (XD 184)

INCLEDON, Charles (1763–1826), tenor, was in the *Beggars Opera* at Covent Garden 1790–1815, and sang in the first performance of Haydn's *Creation* in 1800 (DNB). In the first quarter of that year, he lost his first wife and two daughters, who are buried here along with their three other infant children. (CH 24)

JACKSON, Sir Herbert, KBE, FRS (1863–1936), Emeritus Professor of Chemistry at the University of London; he lived at 9 Parsifal Road. (A 15)

JACKSON, Sara (1910–82), poet. She lived at 2 Prospect Place, overlooking the new graveyard, which she lovingly tended and beautified with flowers and shrubs. (P 95)

JAY, Edward Aubrey Hastings (1869–1950), father of the Rt Hon. Douglas Jay, PC, Labour MP and President of the Board of Trade 1964–7. Trained as barrister, became fund-raising secretary for medical charities. Lived at 20 East Heath Road, and from 1922 at 13 Well Road. (P 61)

JEEVES, Thomas (1743–1812), linen draper, hosier and haberdasher in the High Street. His son was a Manager of the Parochial School and a Philo-Investigist (see p. 48). (XF 040)

JEVON, Thomas (1652–88), 'an eminent comedian and dancing master', says Park. (XL 022)

JOAD, Dr Cyril Edwin Mitchinson (1891–1953), prodigious writer, popular broadcaster, inspiring teacher. Was Head of Philosophy Dept. at Birkbeck College, became famous in the Brains Trust on radio and television. His last book was *The Recovery of Belief* (1952): he had re-converted to Christianity

Dr Joad of the Brains Trust.

after being an agnostic for most of his life. He lived at 4 East Heath Road from 1931–51 and championed mixed hockey on the Heath. (J 91)

JOHNSON, Sir Arthur (1865–1944), solicitor, who became Hampstead's Vestry Clerk (later Town Clerk) in 1893. Retired after 37 years, he was made the first Freeman of Hampstead. He lived at, among other local addresses, 70 Maresfield Gardens, a house called The Wong. (XF 006)

JOHNSTONE, Sir Donald Campbell (1857–1920), Indian Civil Service; Chief Judge, Chief Court, Punjab from 1915. (I 76)

JONES, Peter (died 1829): 'He lived 25 years a

coachman in the family of George Todd, Esq., of Belsize, who in testimony of his services caused this stone to be erected.' (E 16)

JORDAN, Joseph (1786–1873), FRCS, 'of Manchester. He was the Founder of Provincial Schools of Anatomy, many years consulting surgeon to the Manchester Royal Infirmary, also to the Lock Hospital, of which he was one of the Founders'. (A 93)

JOY, David (1825–1903), engineer and naval architect, who invented new valve gear for locomotives; lived at 118 Broadhurst Gardens. (C 66)

KEATS, John (1795–1821) is commemorated in the church by a bust by Anne Whitney, presented in 1894 by American admirers. He first came to Hampstead about 1815, visiting Leigh Hunt in the Vale of Health to discuss the publication of his first sonnets. After lodging with his brother Tom in Well Walk, he lived at Wentworth Place, now called Keats House, 1818–20. During his time there, he was at the height of his poetical powers, notably in the *Ode to a Nightingale*. He is buried in Rome. (CH 45)

KENNEDY, James (1842–1920) retired to Hampstead from the Indian Civil Service and lived at 14 Frognal Lane. In 1906, he published his useful researches into local history – *The Manor and Parish Church of Hampstead*. (B 4)

KEY, Jonathan (1737–1805) owned the Greenhill Estate and died at Mount Grove. His eponymous son lived at Stanfield House. The family made their fortune as wholesale stationers and the son of **John Key** of Denmark Hill was Lord Mayor of London 1830–31. (XE 117)

KINDER, Eliza (1781–1864), daughter of Henry Enfield, who left his name on Enfield House in Windmill Hill. The Kinders, also lived in Windmill Hill and one of them married Henry Sharpe (q.v.) of Admiral's House. (XB 086)

KING, Charles Bean (1873–1928), the junior member of the building firm of that name, founded in 1746. They built many houses in the Well Walk area; their office was at 28 Church Row. (E Bay 1)

KING, Rev. John (1838–78), 'sometime curate of this parish; the second son of the late Joshua King LLD, President of Queens' College, Cambridge'. (A 79)

KING, William (1754–1821), 'Professor of Music, a pious and respected inhabitant of this village'. (C 50)

KIPPIN, Henry (1909–68) was Hampstead's last chimney sweep, born and died at 3 Perrins Court, home of his grandfather, Edmund (1852–1916),

who founded the family firm. Henry's handcart has been preserved at Burgh House. (F 22)

KNOX, Edmund George Valpy (1881–1971), known as E.V. Knox, or Evoe, poet and satirist, Editor of *Punch* 1932–49. He was son of a Bishop of Lahore, and brother of Ronald Knox, the author/priest. He lived many years in Hampstead at 34 Well Walk, and latterly at 110 Frognal. He was active on local committees, notably at the Parochial School, of which he wrote an entertaining history. His features may be seen in Mr Banks of the *Mary Poppins* books, which his wife, Mary, illustrated. (Q 91)

KOCH, Rev. Edward H.A. (1874–1951), Assistant Curate of Parish Church and wrote a brief history of it (1928). He was later Vicar of St Saviour's. Died at 70 Haverstock Hill. (A 31)

LAKE, Ernest Edward (1844–1917), 'for some years churchwarden of this parish' (until 1904), also Mayor of Hampstead 1908. He lived at 1 East Heath Road. (CH 48)

LANE, Rev. Charlton (died 1875), '32 years incumbent of St Mark's, Kennington, and 9 years Vicar of Hampstead' (1864–73). Gave stained glass window (see CH 82) to Sir Thomas Maryon Wilson. (XD 166)

LANGMEAD, William (1812–82), carver, gilder and paperhanger in the High Street, became parish clerk (1851–82), sexton and undertaker. (XF 058)

LANKESTER, Edwin (1814–74), MD, FRS, Coroner for Central Middlesex (1862–74). Lived at 68 Belsize Park. DNB adds: 'Professor of Natural History, New College, London. . . . Published works on physiology and sanitary science.' (E 85)

LE BRETON, Philip H. (1806–84), barrister, Vestryman, Heath defender, Chairman, Metropolitan Board of Works Parks Committee. Cousin of Lily Langtry. Lived in Keats Grove. (XB 124)

LESSINGHAM, Mrs Jane (1739–83) 'late of the Theatre Royal, Covent Garden'. The original inscription added that 'her grateful and affectionate son, William Frederick, caused this tomb to be repaired anno 1802': he was one of four sons who benefited from her will. Mrs Lessingham is less remembered locally as an actress than as an encroacher on the Heath. Her attempts to build Heath Lodge (on the site of the present Hill Garden) brought a law suit against her by other residents in 1775, led by Henry White of XD 149. (XD 221)

LEWER, Henry (1752–1819): 'This tomb was built by Henry Lewer Esq. of Pimlico as a place of rest for the mortal remains of himself and as many of his family as it will contain.' His reason for being buried here was told in an earlier section. (XB 190)

LIVOCK, John, junior (1779–1840), coal merchant (like his father) of Heath Street. Livock's Alley was the name for the western passage from Heath Street to Holly Mount. (XH 019)

LLOYD, John (1746–91) was the only Hampstead body to be involved in body-snatching (q.v. above). (XB 199)

LLOYD, Thomas (1689–1753) 'one of the Attornies in the Exchequer of Pleas . . . he bore an illness of many years continuance with amazing spirit . . .' (XE 046)

LONGMAN, Thomas Norton (1771–1842) 'bookseller and publisher of the City of London, 42 years an inhabitant of this parish. . . . This monument has been erected by his personal friends to record their deep sense of the many excellencies that distinguished his private character and of the advantages conferred on literature by the ability, integrity and enterprise which he displayed as head, for more than half a century, of the first publishing house in the United Kingdom.'

Longman was great-nephew of the eponymous founder of the family firm in Paternoster Row and son of Thomas Longman (1730–97), who came to Hampstead c. 1792. T.N. Longman lived at Manor House, Frognal, from c. 1804 and moved to Mount Grove, Greenhill, c. 1817. Here he entertained Scott, Southey, Coleridge, etc., grew pineapples and other hothouse fruit and died worth £200,000 – after being thrown from his horse in St Pancras (some say Haverstock Hill). The family vault is at Friern Barnet. (CH 87)

LORANT, Louis (1768–1837), 'a native of Normandy, 29 years a Licensed Victualler in this parish'; he was publican of the White Bear in New End, which in the 1830s was 'much frequented by foreigners', says Barratt. (I 51)

LORD, Charles Francis James (1803–91), surgeon and first Medical Officer of Health for Hampstead from 1856. He carried out radical reforms in his roles of Sanitary Inspector, Public Vaccinator and Medical Superintendent of the Workhouse in New End. He lived latterly at Elm Cottage, Rosslyn Hill. His grave includes 2 children and 2 grandchildren, who died in their infancy. (D 76)

LOVELL, Mrs Eleanor (1778–1851) ran a toyshop at 44 High Street, which was also Hampstead's first recorded post office. An 1823 Directory announces 'a letter box at Mrs Eleanor Lovell's from whence the letters are dispatched to London at 9 in the morning and 4 in the afternoon.' (XE 016)

LOVERIDGE, Emilie Muriel (1892–1954), founder and co-principal of St Godric's Secretarial College in Arkwright Road. (Col. N 1)

LOWE, James (1756–1849) 'of Museum St., Bloomsbury and of the East India House, London, who died the 27 August 1849 in the 94th year of his age'. (XD 151)

LYFORD, John (1752–1811), landlord of the Old Bull & Bush, from 1793 until death. (XD 021)

McARDELL, James (1728–65), 'Metzotinto (*sic*) Engraver', e.g. of Reynolds portraits. 'He brought the art of mezzotint engraving to great perfection' (DNB). Grave restored by public subscription 1910. (XB 090)

MACDONELL, Sir John (1845–1921), KCB, Senior Master of Supreme Court and King's Remembrancer, 1912–20, jurist, author and editor of law works. His wife, **Dame Agnes**, 'died St Agnes Eve 1925' was niece of Mary Howitt. (I 72)

McGWIRE, Thomas (1734–1803), 'late of Wimpole Street but, previous to the Revolution in America, Attorney General to the Province (of North Carolina), he died in his lodgings in this Parish . . .' (XD 057)

MACIRONE, George Augustus, 'born 8 January 1834, born again 6 July 1834, died 29 March 1910, son of George, son of Pietro Bonaventura Augusto Gaspari, son of Francesco Filippo Ludovico Melchiori . . .' and 3 other male Italian antecedents. He lived at 126 Adelaide Road. (D Bay 3)

MACKINTOSH, Rt Hon. Sir James (1763–1832), Scots philosopher, barrister, Recorder of Bombay 1804–6, Professor of Law at Haileybury 1818–24, MP for Knaresborough 1819. He died after swallowing a chickenbone. (XB 149)

MAGRATH, Edward (1791–1861), secretary of the Athenaeum Club, lived at Capo di Monte from 1846. He investigated the origin of the name Judges Walk, and saw evidence of Assizes being held on the Heath during the Great Plague. (E 19)

MALDEN, Henry (1800–76), 'for 45 years Professor of Greek in University College London' (from 1831 until his death). Headmaster of UCS 1832–42, described in the school's history (1981) as an 'urbane and gentle scholar . . . poet and champion of Greek Independence'. Died at his home in Belsize Square. (G 45)

MALLARD, Stephen (1757–1822), a plumber and glazier with a shop in the High Street. His elder son, William, was a churchwarden, and his name is on one of the present wardens' staves. His younger son, Richard, according to his tombstone 'met his Fate by bathing in the Middle Pond on Hampstead Heath on the 8th day of September 1804 in the 19th year of his age'. (XD 185)

MALLET, John Lewis (died 1861), 'a citizen of Geneva, long resident in this parish', of Huguenot origin. He was a friend of Pitt and, thanks to the latter's influence, became a clerk in the Audit Office soon after 1800 (DNB), The Mallets lived at Belmont on Greenhill. (CH 72)

MALLORY, Mrs Anne (1711–91) of Church Row, left the church a charity of £100 to buy bread for the poor. (XE 035)

MARDEN, Sarah (1787–1860): 'She was for more than 40 years a valued servant and friend of the family of the late Samuel Hoare Esq. of this parish.' The philanthropic Hoare family of bankers lived at Heath House. (XB 009)

MARIS, Matthew (1839–1917), painter and etcher, born The Hague, exhibited frequently, as did his two brothers, in Britain. He and his long-living local artist friends, **Ernest Fridlander** (1870–1960) and **Beatrix Martin** (1876–1964) are commemorated in a series of linked plaques. (K 53–5)

MARSHALL, Julian (1836–1903), a notable collector of engravings, musical autographs and portraits, and of bookplates. He is also known for his *Annals of Tennis* (1878), 'a work of minute and exhaustive research' (DNB). His wife, **Florence** (1843–1922), was a composer and conductor. (C 74)

MARTIN, John Edward (1822–93), for many years Librarian of the Inner Temple and eldest son of John Martin, bibliographer and librarian at Woburn (DNB). (C 1)

MATHIAS, Vincent (1716–82), Treasurer of Queen Anne's Bounty. Married a member of the Popple family (q.v.). (XB 141)

MATTHEWS, Bert (1884–1970) and his wife Rebecca (1884–1963), 'by whose efforts all charities gained', were Pearly King and Queen of Hampstead for many years. They lived at No. 1 Perrins Court. Bert was rat-catcher for Hampstead Council for 40 years. (I 109)

MAY, Otto (1878–1946), MD, FRCP, Chairman of British Social Hygiene Council, Principal Medical Officer of Prudential Assurance Co. Died at Wellside, Well Walk. (J 63)

MAY, William Charles (1853–1931), sculptor and painter, exhibited at RA. Sculpture included Armada memorial on Plymouth Hoe and busts of George V, Walter Besant (q.v.) etc. He painted a

fresco for St Peter's, Belsize Park. Died at Penn Studio, Rudall Crescent. (H 89–90)

MERIVALE, John Herman (1779–1844), 'of Barton Place near Exeter and Bedford Square, London, one of the Commissioners in Her Majesty's Court of Bankruptcy. . . .' Also scholar and minor poet, says DNB. He was a friend of Joanna Baillie, who lived next door to his parents in Windmill Hill. (CH 3)

MERRY, Captain John (1656–1728), 'formerly an East India Commander, one of the Elder Brethren of Trinity House and many years a Governor of the Hudson Bay Company. These employments he was eminently qualified for by his distinguished knowledge in naval affairs and commerce. The interests of the Company by his application and good conduct were recovered from a low and almost desperate condition to a surprising state of wealth and reputation.' DNB says that Merry sailed in search of the North-West Pasage and discovered and gave his name to Merry's Island. (XD 009)

MEYERSTEIN, Edward Harry William (1889–1952), poet, novelist and biographer; was the subject of a memoir by John Wain in *Sprightly Running*. Did he write his own epitaph?

Memoriae sacrum – ask not who he was!
Transparent was his character as glass;
Words were his love, a verbal grace his aim,
This stone records an unremembered name.
(V 3)

MILLIGAN, Robert (1746–1809), wealthy West India merchant, originator of West India Docks at Poplar, where a statue of him was erected soon after his death (since removed). Lived at Rosslyn House. (XB 169)

MITCHELL, Thomas (1751–99), 'Schoolmaster in this Parish upwards of 23 years'. He was co-founder of a Sunday School and Benefit Society c. 1787. The latter activities were sponsored by the local benevolent club, The Philo-Investigists (see p. 48), of which Mitchell was a member. (XD 190)

MONRO, Frederick R. D'Oyly (died 1966), born about 1880 (he joined the local cricket club in 1896), became a solicitor and was for many years secretary of the Royal Sailors' Daughters' Home in Fitzjohns Avenue – now Monro House, named after him. He wrote a history of the Hampstead Cricket Club (1949), in which it is stated that he was 'a Reptonian, an Oxonian, and no mean cricketer'. He lived the last 40 years of his life at 4 Redington Road. (L 56)

MOODIE, Robert (1753–89), 'late Practitioner of Physic in Nassau in the island of New Providence, Surgeon to the Prince of Wales (?8th) American Regiment'. (XB 054)

MOORE, Leslie Thomas (1883–1957), locally-based architect, who was in practice with Temple Moore (see below) and married his daughter, Mary, but was not a blood relation. Built (and restored) many churches, also hospitals and war memorials. Lived at 18 Church Row. (CH 36)

MOORE, Temple Lushington (1856–1920), church architect. In 1912 enlarged Parish Church with new Choir Vestry and Lady Chapel extension. Articled to George Gilbert Scott, Junior, and later his assistant. Lived at 6 Downshire Hill and later 46 Well Walk. (I 84A)

MORELAND, Richard (1861–1948), churchwarden and benefactor of the Parish Church. The Moreland Hall is named after him. He lived at 33 Frognal. (K 40)

MORT, George Frederick (1873–1918), 'a pioneer of aeroplane engines, he sacrificed his life for his duty', aged 45. (H 6)

MOSELEY, William (1810–86) had premises in Heath Street as an upholsterer and undertaker, traditionally linked professions. (XF 064)

MUDDOCK, Samuel (1749–1809), plumber in the High Street, probably also the Mr Muddock in charge of the Watch in the 1780s. (XB 218)

MUMFORD, Susanna (1733–1800), 'nurse to 10 children of Samuel Gambier Esq. of this place'. Gambier was First Commissioner of the Navy and lived at Carlile House. (XF 021)

NEAL, John (1795–1854), carpenter, builder and undertaker to the Edmonton Union (Workhouse), also publican of the Yorkshire Grey (1840). (XH 038)

NEVINSON, Edward Henry (1785–1856), head of a benevolent Hampstead family, which included H.W. Nevinson, the 'Grand Duke' of war correspondents, and C.R.W. Nevinson, the cubist and war artist. Edward was Paymaster of the Exchequer in 1834, when the old Palace of Westminster was burned down: the fire started in his storerooms. His wife, **Charlotte** (1786–1868) helped found the local Clothing Club and other Poor Relief: she was known as Lady Nevinson. His eldest son, **Edward** (1813–52), a barrister at Lincolns Inn, ran the local Savings Bank and Dispensary. His second son, **George** (1818–1901) and his youngest, **Thomas** (1820–95), were both Registrars of the Archdeaconry of Leicester. (D 1–2)

NEWSON-SMITH, Sir Frank (1879–1971), stockbroker, Lord Mayor of London (1943–4), lived to 92. Also his father, **Henry** (1855–98), 'of 37 Walbrook EC and 25 Avenue Road NW, Member of the Court of Her Majesty's Lieutenancy of the City of London'. (A 21–22)

NOBLE, Sophia (1790–1880) ran a girls' school at 6–7 High Street, which Constable's daughters attended: the artist had a high opinion of it. Miss Noble lived to be 90. (E 24)

NORTON, Lady Elizabeth (died 1715), youngest daughter of the Earl of Gainsborough, created baron by Charles II; 'her virtues appeared in every part of her life, her humility in her grave, which she chose in this place'. (XE 062)

ORAGE, Alfred Richard (1873–1934), journalist, lecturer and editor of *New Age*, 1907–22, and of *New English Weekly* from 1932. Published works on Nietzsche, Consciousness, etc. Lived at 9 The Mount. His grave is marked with his divided circle, which he called 'a picture of man'. (L 95)

PAGE, Edward (1739–1817), bricklayer and plasterer in the High Street, related by marriage to the Clowser family of builders (q.v.). (XB 084)

PARSHALL, Annie (1873–1910), first wife of Horace Field Parshall (1865–1932), Chairman of Central London Railway and expert on electrification of railways; he designed a 3-phase Rotary Converter. The Parshalls lived at 59 Netherhall Gardens. (C 94)

PAXON, George (1762–1840) of the High Street, was auctioneer, undertaker and owner of houses in Hampstead Square and North End. His large family, many of them in the building trade, included **George Kirkham Paxon** (1789–1845), who owned property all over Hampstead. Nos. 7–11 Perrins Lane were called Paxon Cottages. (XE 144 etc.)

PAYNE, George (1767–1819), butcher in the High Street (c.f. John Payne) and churchwarden; his name appears on the notice at the main entrance to the 1812 burial ground. (XB 031)

PAYNE, John (1745–1820), butcher in the High Street. He is buried with 4 wives, all of whom he survived. (XB 013)

PEACOCK, Charles (1815–72) ran a laundry in New End and his mother was presumably the Elizabeth Peacock who made straw hats in Heath Street. (XF 008)

PEACOCK, Joseph (1806–58), 'late of the Bull & Bush, North End'. (XK 004)

PEARSE, John Gardner (1817–86), 'for many years a vestryman of Hampstead'; his memorial was 'erected by public subscription in token of appreciation and esteem'. Pearse was a baker at 3–4 High Street, also a Parcels Delivery Office. (H 86)

PERKINS, Rev. W.H. (1812–85), Curate of Christ Church in the 1850s, when he lived in Keats Grove.

Later 'ten years incumbent of All Saints, Childs Hill'. (XD 182)

PERRIN, Bishop (1848–1934), Assistant Bishop of London from 1929: died at 9 Lyndhurst Road. (A 5)

PHILLOTT, Constance (1842–1931), Associate of Royal Water Colour Society, living many years at 6 Downshire Hill. (C 17)

PIERCE, William (1706–71), surgeon, left money to the Parish Church for a Friday evening lecture, bibles for the poor, and candles for church services; also ten shillings per annum to the local Methodists for the use of the preacher. (XD 114)

PILGRIM, James (1723–1813) of the local family of landowners, who left their name on Pilgrims Lane. James was a Vestryman in the 1780s and had a house in the High Street. In 1805 he was living on Red Lion Hill, probably Rosslyn Hill House. (XB 178)

PITT, James (1679–1763), civil servant and literary gentleman. He is supposed to be the person alluded to as Mother Osborne in Pope's *Dunciad* because his letters to the *London Journal* were signed Osborne. (XD 072)

PLATT, Thomas Pell (1801–52), lived at Child's Hill House and gave his name to Platt's Lane. He was an oriental scholar and librarian of the British and Foreign Bible Society. (XB 214)

POND, James and Mary (died 1813 and 1811), 'many years Master and Matron of the Poorhouse of this Parish'; stone erected by the parish. (XH 025)

POOL, Thomas (1733–1813), chief lessee of the Manor Farm in Frognal from 1785, was authorised by the Lord of the Manor in 1786 to dig sand from the Heath at £150 for one year. (XB 089)

POPPLE, William (1666–1722), Secretary to the Board of Trade, and his son, also **William** (1701–64), Governor of Bermuda. (XB 141)

POTTER, George (1805–99) founded the famous local Auctioneers and Estate Agents in Heath Street. He died at 47 Willow Road, aged 95. (B 26)

POTTER, Herbert George (died 1951), JP, FRICS, Mayor of Hendon, Estate Adviser to Hampstead Garden Suburb; he took over the family firm of estate agents, Potters, in Heath Street, from his father. (Col. E 1)

POWELL, David (1806–82) inherited Powell-Cotton lands in West Hampstead, and Heath Lodge in North End Way. He was a Vestryman and Surveyor of the Highways, and married Grizel, daughter of Samuel Hoare. (CH 90)

POWNALL, John (died 1843), 'of the Six Clerks Office'. These were officers of the Court of Chancery in Chancery Lane, disestablished by a statute of 1841. (K 70)

PRANCE, Robert (1799–1869), JP; head of a family who lived in the Frognal area for many years. His son, **Reginald Heber Prance** (1829–1912), who lived at The Ferns, 23 Frognal Lane, was a great benefactor of St Stephen's and Christ Church. (K 72)

PRICE, Richard Henry (1828–76), publican of King of Bohemia. (A 25)

PRITCHARD, Daniel (1789–1861), 'formerly of Eastcourt, Middlesex', was a butcher in New End; the 1840 Directory shows it as a 'ham and beef shop'. (XD 003). Another member of this family, which had local connections over three centuries, was **Henry** (1828–75), a corn dealer at 28 Heath Street. (B 48)

PURVIS, Mary (1745–1804) and her family were linen drapers in the High Street, later Purvis & Evans. (XD 136)

QUARITCH, Helen (1831–99), wife of Bernard the bookseller, who died at 34 Belsize Grove the same year *but* was buried in Fortune Green cemetery. (C 62)

QUILLER-COUCH, Florence Mabel (died 1924), sister of Sir Arthur, lived at 16 Downshire Hill. (G 32)

RADFORD, Ernest (1857–1919) and his wife **Dollie** (1858–1920), poets and Fabians, with a large literary circle, which included D.H. Lawrence: he portrayed them not unkindly in his novel *Kangaroo*. They put up him and his wife Frieda frequently at 32 Well Walk; they lived previously at 16 East Heath Road. (G 102)

REDFERN, James (1838–76), sculptor, 'his work was ever to the glory of God'. Sculptures included 60 statues for west front of Salisbury Cathedral, 8 Christian Virtues on pinnacle of Albert Memorial, Christ in Majesty at Westminster Chapter House, and St George and Dragon on Crimea memorial outside Westminster Abbey. He lived at Woburn House, Pond Street, then at Lower Mount Cottage, South End Road. (B 14)

REED, Langford (1889–1954), prolific author, journalist (e.g. *Daily Mail*) and limerick writer. Compiled the *Complete Rhyming Dictionary* (1936) and the *Complete Limerick Book*. Came from old Hampstead family; lived at 21 Christchurch Hill. His tombstone bears a double limerick (see p. 42). (D 35)

REED, Thomas (1756–1839), 'many years a respectable builder of this parish'; he is described as a 'bricklayer and plaisterer' in the 1805–7 Directory.

He is buried with 6 sons, who predeceased him. (XB 096)

RICH, Colonel Edmund Tillotson (1874–1937), Royal Engineers, was Director in the Survey of India Dept., working on borders of Persia, Russia, etc., where he mastered many eastern languages (Pashtu, Kachin, etc.). He was a member of the Girdlers' Company and a Freeman of the City of London, 1910. (L 78)

RICHARDSON, Horace (1878–1947), ironmonger of 82 Heath Street, Councillor for Town Ward 1927–37, keen amateur actor and organist. (J 66)

RITCHIE, Lady Anne Isabella Thackeray (1837–1919), elder daughter of Thackeray, sister-in-law of Leslie Stephen, a member of a large literary circle. She wrote many novels and a biographical work about her father and his friends. In 1877 she married her cousin, 15 years her junior, **Sir Richmond Thackeray RITCHIE** (1854–1912), KCB, Permanent Under Secretary of State for India. He died first, and was buried at Hampstead to be near his friend George du Maurier (q.v.). (H 15)

RIXTON, John (c. 1579–1658), a gentleman from Lancashire ('Great Sonky'), who left £3 a year 'for bread to be distributed . . . to ye poorest sort of people inhabiting within this parish upon every Sabboath (*sic*)' His tombstone is the oldest monument to survive here. He lived to about 80, and his wife to about 90. (See inscription in Appendix.) (CH 52 and 74)

ROBERTSON, John Archibald Campbell (1912–62), CB, Under Secretary at the Treasury and from 1954–7 Director of Personnel at the United Nations Headquarters. He died at 18 South Grove, Highgate. (K 17)

ROBOTHAM, Francis Jonathan (c. 1760–1850) was a watchmaker in the High Street and died in his 90th year, 'the oldest inhabitant of this Parish'. His son of the same name (1799–1854) was not only a watchmaker and jeweller, but Agent for Alliance Fire Insurance, Collector of the Queen's Taxes and Highway Rate, Actuary to the Savings Bank, and Registrar of Births, Marriages and Deaths. The 1851 Census shows him owning most of Holly Mount and half of Holly Hill. (XD 078)

ROSE, Dr Henry Cooper (1831–1914), 'Surgeon Major and of the Middle Temple Barrister at Law, who practised as a physician in Hampstead for more than 40 years.' Dr Rose lived at the corner of Rosslyn Hill and Shepherds Walk. (A 12)

ROOTH, Henry Goodwin (1861–1928), West India merchant and ship-owner, barrister, Metropolitan Police Court Magistrate 1917–28. Lived at Weatherall House, Well Walk. (K 30)

ROXBURGH, Archibald Cathcart (1886–1954), physician in charge of the Skin Department, St Bartholomew's Hospital; Dean of London School of Dermatology, author of *Common Skin Diseases* (many editions) etc. Born Valparaiso, died 4 Redington Road. (Col. E 3)

RUMSEY, Thomas (died 1798?) left £1,000 invested in 3% Consolidated Bank Annuities for 'coal or other fuel to be distributed at Christmas in each year to poor families . . . who frequent the established Church of England'. (XB 206)

RYAN, William Patrick (1851–1921), 'Papal Zouave', lived at 18 Ellerdale Road. (Zouaves were 'French Infantry of great dash, originally Algerians, wearing a quasi-Moorish dress' – Chambers' Dictionary) (H 26)

SAMUELSON, Sir Herbert Walter (1865–1952); KBE, Chairman and Treasurer of University College Hospital, 1927–37; he married **Sybil** (née Harbord), OBE (1876–1961). They lived at 2 Greenaway Gardens. (G 105)

SATT, Marie Antoinette (1805–1881), born in Boulogne, died in South Hackney, was buried here, according to her wish, beside her friend and mistress. Her tombstone, all in French, inspired one member of the public to enquire if *the* Marie Antoinette was buried in Hampstead. (D Bay 2)

SATTERTHWAITE, James (1794–1865), one of a large Hampstead family; he is shown in the 1840 Directory both as bricklayer and china dealer! (XD 046 and 113)

SCHWABE, Randolph (1885–1948), artist, Slade professor 1930–48. Member of New English Art Club and London Group. 'His drawings and prints beautifully precise and reasonable statements of fact' (DNB). Lived at 20 Church Row from 1929 until his death. (N 109)

SCOTT, Sir George Gilbert (1811–78), architectural champion of Gothic Revival, designer of Albert Memorial, St Pancras Station Hotel, etc., drastic restorer of churches; lived at Admiral's House 1856–64. His memorial window in church is by 'one sometime his pupil', Alfred Bell. He is buried in Westminster Abbey. (CH 92)

SCOTT, George Gilbert, junior (1839–97), 'FSA, sometime Fellow of Jesus College, Cambridge', architect son of Sir George, father of Sir Giles. Restored several Oxbridge colleges. Associated with Bodley & Garner, and Watts & Co, producing Pre-Raphaelite church fittings. Lived at

26 Church Row. His youngest son **Adrian** (died 1963) was also an architect, e.g. of St Albans, Golders Green. He designed for himself Shepherd's Well, a house in Frognal Way, in 1930. (B 85)

SCOTT, Sir John (1841–1904), KCMG, DCL, 'sometime Judge of the High Court of Bombay, Judicial Adviser to HH the Khedive of Egypt, Deputy Judge Advocate General to HM Forces . . .' His wife **Edgeworth Leonora** (1842–1924), named after Maria Edgeworth, was a niece of Sir Rowland Hill, the postal reformer. Sir John was also linked to the Hill family through his sister and stepmother. (D 91)

SEALY, Captain John (1733–1809), 'formerly Commander in the Hon. East India Company Maritime Service and an Elder Brother of the Corporation of the Trinity House'. (XD 064)

SELWYN, Bishop George Augustus (1809–1878), first Bishop of New Zealand and 90th Bishop of Lichfield, where he died; he was born in Church Row. Selwyn College, Cambridge, was erected in his memory by public subscription in 1882. He and his two distinguished brothers are commemorated on a piscina in the Lady Chapel. (CH 40)

SHAIRP, Alexander Mordaunt (1887–1939), music master at UCS, also a dramatist, whose successes included *Crime at Blossoms* and *The Green Bay Tree* (1933). Lived at 13 Heath Mansions. (P 71)

SHARP, Constance Dorothea (1863–1928), daughter of Priestley Birch, married Cecil Sharp, the folk music champion, in 1893. Their last home was at 4 Maresfield Gardens, which now bears his plaque. He died in 1924 and was cremated at Golders Green. (H 79)

SHARPE, Daniel (1805–56), 'of Broad St Buildings, Portugal Merchant, and Fellow of the Geological Society, of which he was President at the time of his death. He died on the 31st May 1856 in consequence of a fall from his horse.' He wrote important papers on European geology (DNB). (XB 136)

SHARPE, Ven. Ernest Newton (1867–1949), Archdeacon of London 1930–47. From 1894–1908 he was Vicar of Emmanuel Church, West Hampstead. He was son of Rev. Henry Sharpe (see below). (N 62)

SHARPE, Henry (1802–73), Portugal merchant of Fenchurch Street, with his brother Daniel (q.v.); monument in the church 'raised by those who derived benefit in their youth from his disinterested efforts for their instruction and improvement'. He also erected Hampstead's first drinking fountains. The family lived at Admiral's House from 1865. His wife, **Eliza** (died 1901), kept a logbook to the age of 90, which has been preserved in the Sharpe Collection at the Local History Library. (CH 76)

SHARPE, Rev. Henry (1833–1900), 'for 28 years the greatly loved Vicar of Trinity Church, Hampstead, and for 7 years previously Minister of the temporary church, Hampstead Fields'. Sharpe came to Hampstead from the backwoods of Canada to develop the new parish of Holy Trinity, Finchley Road. The temporary Mission Hall was in Belsize Lane, but Sharpe spent some time preaching to the navvies building the railways' Belsize Tunnel, often 60 feet below ground. (XE 085)

SHAW, Richard Norman 1831–1912), RA, champion of the Queen Anne revival in architecture and designer of New Scotland Yard (1888) and the Piccadilly Hotel. He built several local houses, including 39 Frognal for Kate Greenaway and, in 1875, 6 Ellerdale Road for himself: he lived there until his death. He also designed the original version of the Moreland Hall for the Parish Church in 1893. (XB 128)

SHELDON, Harriot (1748–1830) 'was a descendant of Dr Sheldon, the Archbishop of Canterbury, who founded the Theatre of the University of Oxford, and only Survivor of the name. . . .' Her married sister died four years later, aged 92. (D 99)

SHEPHERD, Benjamin (1850–1923) and **Frederick** (died 1941) of the firm of builders, long based at 5 Church Row. They built the Old Town Hall in 1876 and much of Cannon Place the following year (B 39 and 41). **William** (1815–76), the father of the firm, is described as 'plumber, 25 years a tradesman of this parish'. (A 36)

SHERINGHAM, George (1884–1937), landscape and poster artist, illustrator, theatrical and textile designer. Exhibited at RA, Fine Art Society, etc. Works brought by Tate and provincial galleries. Lived at 106 Frognal. (N 92)

SHOUT, Charles Lutwyche (1795–1855), one of a family of sculptors, who lived at Treherne House, West End, Hampstead. His father, Robert (1764–1843), is commemorated in the church, but buried at Kensal Green. Shelley, writing about Leigh Hunt, says that his studio 'no doubt/Is still adorned with many a cast by Shout'. (J 103)

SHUTER, Elizabeth (died 1727) left the church some land in Buckinghamshire to maintain two poor widows in Hampstead. (XE 089)

SIBTHORP, Abraham (1697–1753), an Overseer of the Poor. Each of his two wives 'died in childbed' at an early age; they are buried in adjoining graves. **Thomas** (? his son) was a churchwarden in charge of the Poor Rate in 1774. The family owned property in the High Street, including the King's Arms Tavern. (XE 133)

SINCLAIR, May (1863–1946), novelist, whose *Audrey Craven* in 1896 showed her as a pioneer in the use of stream-of-consciousness technique. She lived locally in Christchurch Hill and Willow Road. (XF 005)

SINTON, George 1787–1846), auctioneer and nurseryman of Haverstock Hill. Four of his family, aged 11–29, died within a few days in May 1842, perhaps because of a cholera epidemic. (G 19–24)

SINTON, Walter (1857–1881), 'late Corporal 1st Royal Dragoons. This wreath and inscription is placed here by his comrades in Hampstead Troop of the above regiment as a mark of their respect' (no trace of wreath now). (XI 024)

SMALLEY, Rev. Cornwall (1790–1859), 'was Vicar of Brailes, Warwick, and afterwards incumbent of St Matthew's, Bayswater, in this County, where a tablet is erected to his memory'. Two of his descendants visited the grave in 1979 and told us that the reverend gentleman, who had 16 children, nearly bankrupted himself on the building costs of St Matthew's. (XB 174)

SMITH, Basil Woodd (1831–1901), presumably a descendant of Basil Woodd (q.v.), was chairman of the local JPs; he lived at Branch Hill Lodge. (XD 197)

SMITH, Trafford (1913–75), CMG; with Colonial Office, posts in Fiji and other islands; Lt./Gov. of Malta 1953–9, Ambassador to Burma 1967–70. from 1970–75 he was Clerk to the Hampstead Wells and Campden Trust. He died at 3 Prince Arthur Road. (Col. E 2)

SNOXELL, Edward (1691–1766) farmed part of the Manor Farm, owned the King's Head (site of William IV), and fields in Kilburn; he was also an Overseer of the Poor. (XG 028)

SOSKICE, Frank, Lord Stow Hill (1902–79), barrister son of a Russian doctor, and grandson of Ford Madox Brown; in 1945 was knighted, made QC and Labour MP for Birkenhead East. Became Attorney General, 1951, Home Secretary 1964–5, and Lord Privy Seal 1965. Lived some 30 years at 19 Church Row. (Q 89–90)

SPEDDING, Anthony (1776–1837), attorney of Norfolk Street, Strand, was partner of Charles Bicknell, Constable's father-in-law, and the artist's

legal adviser. He lived at the Old Court House from 1813 until his death. (J 102)

STAMP, Edward Blanchard (1834–1908), born at Newcastle-on-Tyne, chemist at 29 High Street, still called Stamp's. One of his sons was Deputy Keeper of Public Records and earned a CB. (C 22)

STEPHENSON, Frances (1803–42), wife of the Civil Engineer, Robert Stephenson (1803–59), who built *inter alia* the Euston-Birmingham Railway in the 1830s. He lived in Haverstock Hill 1835–43, and is buried in Westminster Abbey. (J 97)

STEVENSON, Samuel (1773–1855), '35 years parish clerk'; in the 1840 Directory he is shown as Manor Bailiff in Church Row. (XB 116)

STONE, George (1865–1955), policeman at the old police station at the top of Rosslyn Hill; he lived to 90, and died at Willow Buildings. (J 89)

STRIDE, John (1746–1825), 'of Carey Street ... Gentleman ... Steward of the Manor of Hampstead for 43 years'; he was a solicitor and died at the Old Court House. (CH 68)

SUTTON, Tom (1892–1972), 'verger and parish clerk for 39 years and a friend to this church all his life'; he was verger from 1930 and lived at 52 Gayton Road. (CH 35)

SWEENEY, Christopher (1870–1927) lived at 3 Holly Mount and was verger of the parish church for the last 30 years of his life. His funeral attracted 200 mourners. (D 41)

TAIT, Archbishop (1811–82), an influential Archbishop of Canterbury from 1869; not buried here, but he has a memorial window in the church. Among other measures, he strongly supported the Burials Act of 1880, which allowed non-conformists to be buried in churchyards with their own service. (CH 94)

TANCRED, Harriet (died 1864), first wife of Sir Thomas Tancred (1840–1910), mining and railway engineer, contractor for the Forth Bridge. (B 59)

TANNER, Margaret (died 1849), 'beloved wife of John Richard Tanner, confectioner of this parish, who died aged 39 years, leaving 7 children under 12 years of age.' (XF 039)

TAYLOR, Catherine (died 1933), wife successively of two West Hampstead painters – firstly Frank Craig, and secondly Leonard Campbell Taylor, RA: both are widely represented in national galleries, including the Tate. (B 57)

TAYLOR, David (1846–77), 'Master of the Christ Church National School, Hampstead, the friend and elder brother of his boys'; he died aged 31. (A 27)

TAYLOR, Gilbert (1878–1948) ran popular Fried

Fish Shop at 5–7 Flask Walk in 1920s and 30s. (C 28)

TAYLOR, William (1684–1747), 'who was several years one of the pages of the bed-chamber to their Majesties King George the First and Second'. Vainly he tried to be buried inside the church (see story p. 32). (XE 001)

THOMAS, Albert John (1879–1964), architect, e.g. jointly of the Institut Français in Kensington (1939) in Art Nouveau style. He died at 28 Upper Park Road. (J 36)

THOMSON, Dame Julia (died 1722), 'relict of Sir William Blackett of Newcastle upon Tyne, Bart., afterwards wife of Sir William Thomson, Knight, Recorder of the City of London'. She had other noble connections. She was grand-daughter of Sir Richard Lumley and daughter of Sir Christopher Conyers (whose first wife was daughter of William Langhorne, Lord of the Manor of Hampstead). One of her sons married Lady Barbara Villiers and a daughter married David Erskine, 4th Earl of Buchan (q.v.) (XD 081)

THOMPSON, Sir Matthew William (1872–1956), 3rd Baronet, FRAS, painter, died at 39 Steele's Road. Grave bears the family crest and motto: 'Wheare virtue lys, love never dys'. (I 91)

THORPE, Thomas Wells (c. 1851–1943), as chairman of Mann, Crossman & Paulin, he introduced many technical changes in brewing methods. He was a co-founder of the Van Horse Parade in Regents Park. Lived at 52 Redington Road from 1908 until his death at 92. (P 86)

TIDEY, Daniel (c. 1815–82) was landlord of the Washington Hotel, Englands Lane, and of the Belsize Tavern. He is buried with **Eliza Tidey**, the mother of his children, but not officially his wife. (B 87)

TODD, Ernest (1861–1914), JP, Alderman and Mayor of Hampstead 1910–11. Lived at 157 Haverstock Hill. (F 99)

TODD, George (1762–1829) 'of Bellsize' (*sic*), a Baltic merchant, who made a fortune and acquired a wife in Riga. He owned part of the Belsize House Estate and lived at Ivy Bank on Haverstock Hill. (CH 58 and K 105)

TOLLER, Thomas (1800–79) was a solicitor, Clerk to Hampstead Vestry, 1832–68, Clerk to the Guardians, Superintendent Registrar, and Secretary to the Copyholders Committee, who fought the Heath battle against the Lord of the Manor. He lived at (old) 36 Well Walk, next to the Pump Room. His father lived at Admiral's House. (A 98)

TOMLIN, William (died 1887), 'for 34 years a city missionary at Hampstead. A good soldier of Christ.' (F 46)

TOOLEY, George (1792–1876) ran a laundry at North End. His son (?) **Thomas** (1816–1900) was '50 years Job and Fly Master of this parish'. His carrying business at 8 Heath Street was established in 1835. Another **Thomas** (1840–1929), probably his son, was a dairyman at North End and ran Wildwood Farm. (H40, XG 008, G 41)

TOTHILLS, Jane (1770–1845), one of several servants of the Mallet and Merivale families (q.v.) buried together. Jane lived in for nearly 25 years. **Joseph Sparkes** (died 1850) was 16 years a gardener, and **Jane Slee** (died 1874) 'after long and faithful service, retired on her own means and lived to the age of 90, respected by all'. (B 93)

TOUT, Thomas Frederick (1855–1929), historian and teacher, Fellow of Pembroke College, Oxford, Professor at Lampeter and later Manchester (1890–1925). He published numerous textbooks, specialising in mediaeval history (DNB). Chaucer supplied the epitaph on his grave: 'And gladly wolde he lerne and gladly teche.' According to the magazine of the Historical Association, of which he was President 1910–12, he could be so sharp-tongued that not everyone believed that 'Tout comprendre c'est Tout pardonner'. (F Bay 1)

TOWLE, Sir William (1849–1929), KB; was noted for improving railway refreshments – for many years he was manager of Midland Railway Hotels. He lived at 52 Fitzjohns Avenue. One of his sons, **Sir Francis** (1876–1951), CBE, was Managing Director of Gordon Hotels, and the other, **Arthur** (1878–1948), CBE, controlled LMS Hotel services: the latter married Margery Lawrence, author of *Madonna of the Seven Moons*. (A 74)

TOWNER, Grace (1862–1949), mother of the local landscape artist, Donald Towner (died 1985), with whom she lived for many years in Church Row. The inscription aptly includes 'The Grace of our Lord Jesus Christ be with you'. (XF 007)

TRAILS, John (1705–67) of Crediton, 'who lived at the Halfway House in Hampstead Road'; this was on the site of Camden Town Tube Station. (XG 023)

TREE, Sir Herbert Beerbohm (1853–1917), actor-manager, Haymarket Theatre, 1887–97, when he built Her Majesty's. Founded RADA 1904, knighted 1909. He lodged in Haverstock Hill in the 1880s and lived grandly at The Grange, Branch Hill, 1890–91. One of his 3 daughters, the actress Viola (Parsons), who died in 1938, is buried next to him in F 2. The film director, Carol Reed, was his natural son. (G Bay)

TYLER, Evan (died 1682), so-called Prince Tyler, was Master of the Stationers' Company in 1672; his is one of the two 17th-century graves that have survived. (XE 068)

UNDERHILL, Evelyn (1875–1941), religious writer, poet and mystic. Served in Admiralty intelligence in World War I but became pacifist. She was much influenced by Baron Friedrich von Hügel, who lived in Hampstead, and 'she devoted herself to giving spiritual direction, retreats, etc.' (DNB). She often stayed with her friend, Mrs Vernon, at 12 Hampstead Square, and here she died. (P 80)

VALENTINE, Susannah (1804–30): 'She was mistress of the National School of this Parish upwards of 10 years. Her zealous labour in which situation caused her death, when Society lost an exemplary Christian and Hampstead a valuable servant.' As she died aged 26, she began teaching at 16. The National became the Hampstead Parochial School. (E 2)

VAUGHAN, Tom (1871–1929), was Business Manager to Sir Gerald du Maurier, notably during his management of Wyndham's Theatre, 1910–25. After Vaughan's early death Sir Gerald had little success, according to his daughter Daphne. Vaughan lived at 172 Haverstock Hill. (B 22)

VINCENT, John, senior (1664–1719) had a brewery in the High Street around 1700, and laid water pipes thither from the Cold Bath near Well Road. He also brought the first piped water to other Hampstead residents. He ran Jack Straw's Castle c. 1713. His son rebuilt the brewery in 1720, as the arch next to 9A High Street says. His grandson, **Robert** (1729–86), owned Nos. 3–17 High Street, two pubs (now gone) and the pond in Well Road. (XB 164)

WAAD, Armigell (c. 1510–68), Chief Clerk of the Privy Council to Henry VIII and Edward VI; his earlier voyage to Newfoundland had earned him the title of 'the English Columbus'. He died at Belsize House, but his 'fine alabaster monument' (Park) in the church has gone. (See inscription in Appendix.) (CH 97)

WALBROOK, Anton (1896–1967), actor on stage and screen. Born in Vienna, son of Adolph Wohlbrück, a famous clown. Abandoned successful stage career in Germany because of Nazi regime and settled in England, 1936. Helped many of his countrymen to escape from Europe. First London stage production was *Design for Living* (1939), and the last *Call Me Madam* (1948). Films included *Sixty*

Glorious Years and *La Ronde*. From 1960 until his death he lived at 69 Frognal. His grave (picture on page 10) includes the ashes of his devoted secretary for 23 years, **Eugene Edwards**, who died in 1970. (J 1)

WALKER, Louisa (1853–1922), 'for 44 years Headmistress of Fleet Road Infant School'; she died at 15 Tanza Road. (I 102)

WALLER, Charles (1868–1956), coachman to Lord Glendyne, first at Hendon Hall, then at Branch Hill Lodge from 1900. (J 85)

WALLIS, Taverner (1712–79), was descended from the eminent mathematician, John Wallis (1616–1703), who revealed the value for Π, invented the infinity symbol, ∞, and founded the Royal Society. (XE 158)

WALTERS, Aaron (1833–94) from Devon is described as 'architect, etc.' in the 1873 Directory; he was then living near Boundary Road. His grave records the loss of 4 children in infancy, including twins. (XB 019)

WARE, Robert (1814–84), publican of successively the Three Horseshoes and Jack Straw's Castle. (C 24)

WARREN, Rev. Robert (1680–1740), Vicar of Hampstead, 1735–40 'and of St Mary le Bow in Middlesex'; also his son, Rev. **Langhorne Warren** (1711–62), who took over the parish from his father in 1740 until his early death. During his tenure the new parish church was built, 1745–7; he was also Vicar of Dedham. (XB 024)

WASH, Henry (1825–1913) lived at 41 Downshire Hill and was in charge of the Church School in that road. He also contributed much information to Baines's *Records of Hampstead* (1890). (XD 044)

WATSON, George (1757–1809) and his eponymous son were blacksmiths, whitesmiths and ironmongers in the High Street for many years; the son was also a churchwarden. (XD 144)

WATSON, Dame Johanna (1754–1811), 'widow of Sir James Watson, Kt., late one of the Judges of the Supreme Court of Judicature at Bengal'. Sir James was the son of a dissenting pastor in Southwark; he became ordained, but forsook the cloth for the law. A protégé of Lord Mansfield, he became MP for Bridport and was knighted on becoming Chief Justice of India in 1794. (XB 180)

WATSON, Thomas Henry (1839–1913), FRIBA, architect of St. Luke's, Deptford (1872) etc. He lived at 5 Akenside Road. (D 83)

WATTS, Arthur George (1883–1935), cartoonist with *Punch* from 1911 and illustrated *Both Sides of the Microphone* for *Radio Times* from 1928. The attic of 1 Holly Place was his studio 1911–35. He married Marjorie Dawson Scott, daughter of the founder of the PEN Club, as his second wife. He was killed in a civil air crash, July 1935. (N 79)

WATTS, George (died 1746), Curate of Hampstead for 49 years. (XL 028)

WATTS, Henry (1815–84), FRS, chemist, Professor of University College, editor of Dictionary of Chemistry (1868): lived at 151 King Henry's Road (DNB). (C 72)

WATTS, William Huson (1822–1907), 'for 65 years resident in Hampstead', a builder, who erected and lived at 15 Perrins Lane, and monumental mason (e.g. CH 89). (A 106)

WAUGH, Arthur (1866–1943), managing director of publishers Chapman & Hall (1902–30), and father of Alec and Evelyn Waugh. The family lived at 11 Hillfield Road, 1878–1907, and at 145 North End Road, 1908–33. The motto on his grave: 'And another book was opened, which is the Book of Life'. (F 18)

WEDGWOOD, Hensleigh (1803–91), philologist, published first etymological dictionary (1857); grandson of Josiah of Etruria. (XB 149)

WENTWORTH, Captain Frederick Charles Ulick Vernon (1866–1947), RN, CB, JP, Director of Mann Egerton & Co., High Sheriff of Suffolk, 1912. Died at 47 Redington Road. (He appears in *Who Was Who* as Vernon-Wentworth, but there is no hyphen on the gravestone.) (M 104)

WEST, Canon Edward Courtenay (1872–1938), was Canon in Cape of Good Hope and, from 1934, of Salisbury Cathedral. From 1929 he was Principal of St Boniface College, Warminster, where he died. (L 106)

WESTALL, William (1781–1850), ARA, topographical painter (sample in the Tate Gallery), draughtsman to Matthew Flinders on his Australian expedition, busy illustrator of topographical works (DNB). Barratt says he painted several Hampstead scenes, but no other local connection found. In October 1985, a Westall view of Sydney was sold there by Sotheby's for £77.295. (XD 129)

WHITE, Henry (1735–1807) and his son of the same name were builders and property owners in the Holly Hill area. They also fought the Lord of the Manor over the Heath. In 1780 the father led copyholders in a successful claim to be able to dig sand and gravel on the Heath. In 1829, the son was among the first to oppose the Lord's development plans. (XD 149).

WHITE, Rev. Samuel (1766–1841), DD, Vicar of Hampstead from 1807–41. His father, the rich squire of Hoddesdon Hall in Oxfordshire, bought the living for him. White put his curates to live in the old vicarage at 28 High Street and took up a grander residence in Montagu Grove. According to Kennedy, 'Dr White preferred the open country of Frognal to the town'. (XH 039 and CH 2)

WHITEING, Richard (1841–1928), 'author of *No. 5 John Street* and other works': the former was filmed in 1921. Whiteing was also a successful journalist. In 1869 he married the niece of the first U.S. Minister to Japan (DNB). He died at 35A High Street. (K 32)

WHORWOOD, Abigail (no date), wife of John Whorwood of Stourton Castle, and daughter of Sir William Waad, Knight, of Belsize, son of Armigell Waad (q.v.). (XL 028)

WILLIAMS, Neville John (1924–77), FRHistS, FSA, Deputy Keeper of PRO 1970–73, Secretary of British Academy 1973–77. His publications included many studies of the Tudor period. He died at 57 Rotherwick Road, NW11. (Col. E 2)

WILLOUGHBY, Dobson (1768–1833), a distinguished lawyer of Cliffords Inn. From 1804 he and his wife, **Sarah** (1776–1833), lived at Ivy Bank, Haverstock Hill. Their second son, Benjamin, married Janet, daughter of Edward Carlile (q.v.). The family is commemorated in Willoughby Road, on what was the Carlile Estate. (CH 61)

WILSON, Sir John Maryon (1802–76), 9th Baronet, brother and heir to Sir Thomas (q.v.). Sir John came to terms with the Metropolitan Board of Works and sold them his rights in the Heath in 1871 for £45,000. (CH 88)

WILSON, Sir Thomas Maryon (1800–69) is commemorated by a stained glass window in the church; it was dedicated to him by the vicar, Charlton Lane, in 1869, who was doubtless grateful to him for his appointment. Maryon Wilson, the 8th Baronet, was the Lord of the Manor, usually known as 'the villainous Lord', who tried for 40 years to build on the Heath. The family lived at Charlton in Kent. (CH 82)

WOODD, Basil George (1781–1872), prosperous wine merchant of New Bond Street, was called 'the father of the London wine trade'. He came to Hampstead in 1826 and later (1841) built himself a grand house, Hillfield, in Belsize Park (site of Old Town Hall). His sons, Charles and Robert, were great benefactors of St Stephen's, Rosslyn Hill. (XD 200)

WOODS, Ann (1784–1828), wife of William Woods, the builder, who developed the Downshire Hill area, including St John's (1821–2), and built

houses in the Vale of Health. (XB 014)

WOODS, Sir William (1787–1842), KH, Garter Principal King of Arms. Lived at Lauriston Lodge, near West End Green. (CH 56)

WRAITH, Rev. James (1734–1815), '20 years Pastor of the Independent Congregation in this Town'; he ministered to local Methodists in 'some kind of shed' (says Park) in the Little Church Row area. (XD 105)

WYLD, William (1662–1735), 'late of London, Founder of Bells for Watches and Musical Clocks'. (XB 029)

APPENDIX A: Inscriptions in full

JOHN CONSTABLE (XC 002)

North side: Sacred to the memory of **Maria Elizabeth Constable**, wife of John Constable, Esq., RA, and daughter of Charles Bicknell, Esq., Solicitor to His Majesty George IV, and to the Admiralty. She was born Jany. 15 1787, and died Novr. 23 1828, leaving seven infant children to lament her loss, in common with their surviving parent.

Eheu! quam tenui e filo pendet
Quid-quid in vita maxime arridet

John Constable, Esq., RA, many years a resident in this parish. He was born at East Bergholt in Suffolk, June 11 1776, and died in London March 31 1837. Also of **John Charles Constable**, Esq., of Jesus College, Cambridge, their eldest son. He died March 20 1841, aged 23. His mortal remains are interred in the chapel of his college.

East side: Also to the memory of **Emily**, youngest daughter of John and Maria Constable, who died May 10 1839, aged 14 years. Also in memory of **Alfred Abram Constable**, their third son. He died November 19 1853, aged 27 years. **Isabel Constable**, their second daughter, born August 2 1828, died August 18 1888.

West side: **Charles Golding Constable**, Captain in Her Majesty's (late) Indian Navy, born 29 March 1821, died 18 March 1879, second son of John and Maria Elizabeth Constable. Also **Maria Louisa Constable**, their eldest daughter, born 19 July 1819, died 17 April 1885. Also **Lionel Bicknell Constable**, their youngest son, born 8 January 1828, died 20 June 1887.

PHILADELPHIA HANCOCK (XB 211)

This stone was reported in 1977 to be in poor condition, with 70% of the inscription eroded. In 1981 it was re-cut, with a shortened epitaph, at the expense of the Jane Austen Society. The full version of the original inscription is given below:

In memory of **Philadelphia**, wife of Tysoe Saul Hancock, whose moral excellence united the practice of every Christian virtue. She bore with pious resignation the severest trials of a tedious and painful Malady, and expired on the 26 Feby 1792 aged 61. Also in memory of her grandson, **Hastings**, only child of Jean Capot, Comte de Feuillide, and of Elizabeth his wife, born 25 June 1786, died 9 Oct. 1801. Also in memory of **Elizabeth**, wife of H.T. Austen, Esq., formerly widow of the Comte de Feuillide, a woman of Brilliant, Generous & Cultivated Mind, Just, Disinterested & Charitable. She died after long and severe suffering on the 25 Ap. 1813 aged 50, much regretted by the wise & good, & deeply lamented by the Poor.

JOHN HARRISON (XE 007)

North side:

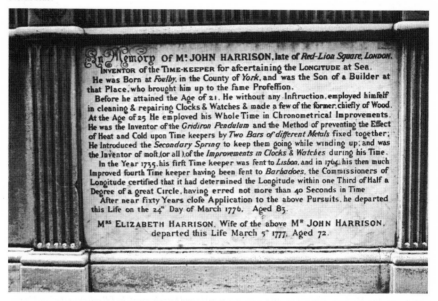

South side: And to his son, **William Harrison**, FRS, born 1728 at Barrow-on-Humber, died 1815. He was the custodian of his father's prize-winning watch H.4. during the vital official trials at sea to Jamaica in 1761, and to Barbados in 1764. He also actively helped his father in the long and difficult negotiations with the Board of Longitude and Parliament when claiming the £20,000 prize. For many years he was a Prominent Governor of the Foundling Hospital, teaching music to the children, and was appointed High Sheriff of Monmouthshire in 1791.

Edge of top slab: Reconstructed at the expense of the Worshipful Company of Clockmakers of the City of London 1879: William Parker, Master. Renewed and the railings removed 1934.

JOHN HINDLEY (XG 001)

Here lie the ashes of **Mr John Hindley**, of Stanhope Street, May Fair, London, originally of King Street, Liverpool, who under peculiar Disadvantages, which to common minds would have been a bar to any exertions, raised himself from all obscure situations of birth and fortune by his own industry and frugality to the enjoyment of a moderate competency. He attained a peculiar excellence in penmanship and drawing, without the instructions of a master, and to eminence in arithmetic, the useful and higher branches of the mathematics, by going to school only a year and eight months. He died a bachelor on the 24th day of October 1807, in the 55th year of his age, and, without forgetting relations, friends or acquaintances, bequeithed (*sic*) one fifth of his property to public charities. Reader, the world is open to thee, go thou and do likewise.

JOHN RIXTON (CH 74)

This tablet on the wall of the north porch must once have been near Rixton's tombstone in the north transept

Be it for ever remembered, to the only praise and glorie of God, who made ye said **John Rixton** an instrument to give by his last Will three pounds a yeare for the good of the poore of this parish of Hampstead, for ever to be paid by the owners of the house wherein Mr Netmaker now dwelleth in Hampstead Streete; and his Will is y^t two pounds twelve shillings thereof shal be paid at ye end of every yeare after his decease for bread to be distributed by the Churchwardens of this parish for the time being, to ye poorest sort of people inhabiting within this parish upon every Sabboath daie by twelve pennyworth every Sabboath yearly for ever, and ye other eight shillings (residue thereof) he giveth to him y^t shalbe Clark of this church for ye time being, yearly to be paid him on every Christmas Day for ever, provided that he (or some other for him) do yearly keepe these two marble stones clean from wet & dust wth wiping them so oft as neede is, otherwise this eight shillings to be given to some other y^t will and doth yearly perform ye same.

ARMIGELL WAAD (CH 97)

Memoriae Sacrum, optimis et charissimis parentibus **ARMIGELLO WAADO**, E Brigantium antiqua familia oriundo; Hen. VIII & Edw. VI Regum secretiori concilio ab epistolis; & in agro Middlesexiano eirenarchae; qui in maximarum artium disciplinis, prudentiaque civili instructissimus, plurimarum linguarum callentissimus, legationibus honoratissimis perfunctus, et inter Britannos Indiarum Americarum explorator primus. Ex duabus conjugibus, Alicia Patencia et Anna Merburia, 20 liberos progenuit, tandemque, post vitam honorifice et pientissime defunctam, anno virginei partus, 1568, mensis Junii die 20 in Domino placide obdormuit. Et **ALICIAE PATENCIAE** quae patri 17 liberos peperit, e quibus duo mares et tres femellae adhuc in vivis existunt, quae vita castissime et temperatissime transacta, anno salutis humanae 1568 animam pientissimam Redemptori reddit. GULIELMUS WAADUS, filius maximus, natus, & haeres, idemque divae Elizabethae reginae concilio secretiori ab epistolis, hoc monumentum posuit.

*(Sacred to the memory of the best and dearest of parents, **Armigell Waad (Wade)**, descended from an old Yorkshire family, Clerk of the Council to Henry VIII and Edward VI; and Justice of the Peace in the County of Middlesex; who was highly cultured, most learnedly versed in civil law, fluent in many languages, a trusted ambassador, and the first British explorer of the American Indies. He begot 20 children by his two wives, Alice Patten and Ann Merbury, and at last, after a life honourably and piously spent, he fell asleep in the Lord in the year of the Virgin Birth 1568, on the 20th day of June. And to the memory of **Alice Patten**, who bore their father 17 children, of whom two males and three females are now living, and who, having spent her life in temperance and chastity, gave her pious soul back to her Redeemer in the year of man's salvation 1568. **William Wade**, their eldest son and heir, himself also Clerk of the Council to the divine Queen Elizabeth, has caused this monument to be erected.)*

APPENDIX B:

Sculptors and other artists

G.G. Adams, CH 76
Robert Ashton, CH 67
John Bacon, Junior, CH 13, 16, 17, 77
J. Bedford, CH 75
Clement Burlison, CH 33
Alan Breese, CH 36, 37, 53
Robert Brown, CH 95
Clayton & Bell, CH 15 etc.
Thomas Denman, CH 91
Alan Lydiat Durst, N 109
John Field, CH 64, 80
Joan Fulleylove, CH 41
Harry Furse, A 66
Thomas Gaffin, CH 70
W. Groves, CH 2

Hart Son Peard & Co., CH 43, 47–9
Humphrey Hopper, CH 62
A.E. Howard, CH 73A
Jones & Willis, CH 39, 44
J. Kendrick, CH 20
Christopher Moore, CH 87
Leslie Moore, I 84A
Patent Works, CH 61
Sir George Gilbert Scott, CH 73
Reynolds Stone, H 4
Donald Towner, CH 39B
William Watts, CH 89
Richard Westmacott (elder), CH 9
Sir Richard Westmacott, CH 58
Anne Whitney, CH 45

A list of masons and undertakers mentioned on the monuments has been lodged with the Local History Library.

APPENDIX C:

Place Names

At the Local History Library at Swiss Cottage, there is an index of all the place names mentioned in the monumental inscriptions. Most North London boroughs are included, and also these localities south of the Thames:

Battersea	Denmark Hill	Lambeth	Putney
Blackheath	Fulham	Old Kent Road	Sydenham
Camberwell	Greenwich	Peckham	Twickenham
Clapham	Kennington	Penge	

All the counties of England are represented – with Yorkshire and Devon surprisingly in the lead – and many corners of Wales and Scotland.

Foreign names abound, of which this a small selection of those not mentioned elsewhere in this book:

Antigua	Haiti	Madras	St Domingo
Bahia	Hawaii	Moscow	St Helena
Baltimore	Hongkong	Nassau	St Petersburg
Bangalore	Hyderabad	New York	Sudan
Borneo	Jamaica	Nova Scotia	Transvaal
Dickebusch	Java	Penang	

BIBLIOGRAPHY

Anon.:	*Church Recorders' Manual* (NADFAS 1982)
Anon.:	*Hampstead at War* (Carlile House 1977)
F.E. Baines (ed.):	*Records of Hampstead* (Whitaker 1890)
Thomas Barratt:	*The Annals of Hampstead* (Black 1912)
Frederick Burgess:	*English Churchyard Memorials* (SPCK 1963)
Rupert Gunnis:	*Dictionary of British Sculptors 1660–1851* (Abbey Library 1968)
Jeremy Jones:	*How to record graveyards* (Council for British Archaeology 1976)
James Kennedy:	*The Manor and Parish Church of Hampstead* (Mayle 1906)
Edward Koch:	*The Parish Church of St John, Hampstead* (SPCK 1928)
Kenneth Lindley:	*Of Graves and Epitaphs* (Hutchinson 1965)
Daniel Lysons:	*Environs of London* (1796)
John Morley:	*Death, Heaven and the Victorians* (Studio Vista 1971)
John James Park:	*The Topography and Natural History of Hampstead* (Nichols 1814)
J.L. Rayment	*Notes on the Recording of Monumental Inscriptions* (Fed. Family Hist. Socs. 1976)
Stapleton/Burman:	*The Churchyards Handbook* (CIO 1976)
Christopher Wade:	*The Streets of Hampstead* (High Hill Press 1984)
Andrew J. Wager:	*Three Centuries of Death* (Trans. S. Staffs. Arch. Soc. 1979)
Caroline White:	*Sweet Hampstead* (Elliot Stock 1901)
H. Leslie White:	*Monuments and their Inscriptions* (Soc. of Genealogists 1977)

Other information from Census Returns, Street Directories, Burial Registers, *Camden History Reviews*, *Who Was Who*, NADFAS, the *Hampstead & Highgate Express*, and the *Dictionary of National Biography*.

CAMDEN HISTORY SOCIETY

Formed in 1970, Camden History Society studies and records the fabric of life in Camden's past, which embraces the old boroughs of Hampstead, St Pancras, Holborn, and the districts of Highgate, Kentish Town and Camden Town.

The Society arranges monthly lectures about local history, and outings in the summer. An illustrated bi-monthly Newsletter is sent to all members, as well as the Society's annual magazine, *Camden History Review*.

Details of membership are available from the Secretary, Camden History Society, c/o Swiss Cottage Library, Avenue Road, London, NW3 3HA.

For a list of the Society's many other publications, apply to CHS Publications, 28 Willoughby Road, London, NW3 1SA.

View across the old churchyard, with Norman Shaw's tomb on the right and the architect's own house in the background.

INDEX

(See also lists in Appendices B and C)
* An asterisk indicates an illustration

92

The du Maurier deadboard, with the Llewelyn Davies grave behind.